WRITERS AND TH

ISOBEL ARMST
General Edi

GEORGE ORWELL

ORWELL AT THE BBC

A photograph of George Orwell broadcasting at the BBC in 1943. From the George Orwell Archive held at University College London, by courtesy of the BBC.

W

GEORGE ORWELL

Douglas Kerr

First published in 2003 by Northcote House Publishers Ltd, Horndon, Tavistock, Devon, PL19 9NQ, United Kingdom.
Tel: +44 (01822) 810066. Fax: +44 (01822) 810034.

British Library Cataloguing-in-Publication Data
A catalogue record for this book is available from the British Library

ISBN 0-7463-1015-3 hardcover
ISBN 0-7463-0972-4 paperback

Typeset by TW Typesetting, Plymouth, Devon
Printed and bound in the United Kingdom by
Athenaeum Press Ltd., Gateshead, Tyne & Wear

Contents

Acknowledgements

I am very grateful to Isobel Armstrong, the general editor of this series, for inviting me to write about Orwell. My warmest thanks for their help to Geetanjali Chanda and Nicola Nightingale. I am also much indebted in various ways to Elaine Ho, Patricia Aske, Thomas Healy, and John E. Joseph. I was glad of a grant from the Hong Kong University Committee for Research and Conference Grants. Like anyone else who has an interest in Orwell, I have reason to be most grateful to Peter Davison, heroic editor of the twenty volumes of Orwell's *Complete Works*.

Biographical Outline

1903	Eric Arthur Blair born, 25 June, in Motihari, Bengal, son of Richard Blair, of the Opium Department, Indian Civil Service, and Ida Blair, née Limouzin.
1904	Ida Blair takes Eric and his elder sister Marjorie back to England. They go to live at Henley-on-Thames, Oxfordshire.
1907	Richard Blair home on three months' leave.
1908	Eric's younger sister Avril born.
1911	In September Eric is sent to St Cyprian's, a private preparatory school at Eastbourne, Sussex, and remains there as a boarding pupil until December 1916.
1912	Richard Blair retires from the Indian Civil Service. The Blair family moves to Shiplake, Oxfordshire.
1914	Outbreak of the First World War. Eric Blair's poem, 'Awake! Young Men of England', printed in the *Henley and South Oxfordshire Standard*.
1915	The family moves back to Henley.
1917	In May Eric goes to Eton College as a King's Scholar.
1921	In December Eric leaves Eton. The Blairs move to Southwold in Suffolk.
1922	In October Eric Blair begins his service with the Indian Imperial Police in Burma, at a starting salary of £444 plus bonuses. After training in Mandalay, he is sent to serve in six different postings, for periods of from four to nine months, his salary rising to £696 plus bonuses.
1927	Returns to Southwold on home leave in September. Resigns from the Burma police. Moves to Portobello

	Road, Notting Hill, London. Early expeditions to the East End of London to examine the conditions of the poor, unemployed and homeless.
1928	Expeditions on the road as a tramp in southern England early in this year. Goes to live in Paris, in the rue du Pot de Fer. Writes several articles published in Paris and London, and either one or two novels. The novels have not survived.
1929	Ill in the Hôpital Cochin in March. In autumn, having run out of money, he works as a dishwasher and hotel porter in a luxury hotel.
1930	Back in his parents' home in Southwold, with excursions tramping and living with down and outs in London. Working on 'Days in London and Paris', and writing essays for the *Adelphi* with the encouragement of Richard Rees.
1931	National Government formed, August. Hop picking in Kent in the autumn. Starts writing *Burmese Days*.
1932	Schoolmaster at The Hawthornes, a boys' school in Hayes, Middlesex, for a year.
1933	Hitler comes to power in Germany. *Down and Out in Paris and London*, by George Orwell, published in January by Victor Gollancz. Teaching for a term at Frays College in Uxbridge, Middlesex. In hospital with pneumonia in December.
1934	*Burmese Days* published by Harpers in New York in October (and by Gollancz in London the following June). Orwell living in a room in Hampstead and working as a part-time assistant at Booklovers' Corner.
1935	*A Clergyman's Daughter* published by Gollancz. Increasing volume of journalistic work.
1936	From January to March, travels in the north of England to collect material for a book on conditions in the depressed areas, commissioned by Gollancz. Moves to The Stores, Wallington, Hertfordshire, in April. *Keep the Aspidistra Flying* published by Gollancz. Marriage to Eileen O'Shaughnessy, June. Outbreak of the Spanish Civil War, June. At Christmas, Orwell leaves for Spain.

1937	Enlists in the POUM militia in January, and fights with the Republican forces on the Aragón front. *The Road to Wigan Pier* published in England by Gollancz in March, and selected as a Left Book Club title. Eileen working in the POUM offices in Barcelona. On leave from the front in Barcelona in April–May, Orwell is caught up in the street fighting between the Communist and anarchist forces. Wounded in the throat by a Fascist sniper on the Huesca front, returns to Barcelona to find the POUM suppressed and many of his friends jailed or murdered. Escapes with Eileen across the border to France in June. Back in England, involved in much journalistic controversy about the events in Spain.
1938	*Homage to Catalonia* published by Secker & Warburg, after being refused by Gollancz. Orwell joins the Independent Labour Party. Munich crisis, September. Orwell spends seven months in French Morocco, for reasons of health, September till the following March.
1939	*Coming Up for Air* published by Gollancz. Richard Blair dies. Outbreak of war with Germany, September. Orwell quits the Independent Labour Party because of its opposition to the war.
1940	First contributions to Cyril Connolly's journal *Horizon*. *Inside the Whale and Other Essays* published by Gollancz. Orwell moves back to London, to Regent's Park, and joins the Home Guard. Heavy aerial bombardment of London (the Blitz) begins in August.
1941	First contribution to the American *Partisan Review*. *The Lion and the Unicorn* published by Secker & Warburg. The Orwells move to St John's Wood. In August, Orwell begins work as Talks Assistant (later Talks Producer) in the Indian Section of the Eastern Service of the British Broadcasting Corporation (BBC). Japan enters the war in December.
1942	Japanese military successes in Asia threaten India. Orwell writing features and regular newsletters, and producing programmes, for the Eastern Service of the BBC. The Orwells move to Maida Vale, London.

1943 Ida Blair dies. Orwell heavily engaged in radio and print journalism. In November, he leaves the BBC, joins *Tribune* as Literary Editor, and begins *Animal Farm* (finished the following February). Begins his personal column, 'As I Please', in *Tribune*.

1944 An infant son, Richard, adopted in June. The Orwells' flat bombed; further moves, to Baker Street, then Islington. Writing for *Tribune, Horizon, Manchester Evening News, Partisan Review*, etc.

1945 From February to March, war correspondent for the *Observer* and the *Manchester Evening News* in France and Germany. In March Eileen Blair dies unexpectedly during a hospital operation. In April Orwell returns to France, Germany, and Austria as a war correspondent. War in Europe ends in May. Orwell working on his new novel in June. Labour government elected in Britain in July. Rejected by many publishers including Gollancz and Faber, *Animal Farm* finally published in August by Secker & Warburg, and becomes a best-seller. First visit to the Scottish island of Jura in September.

1946 *Critical Essays* published by Secker & Warburg. More non-fiction, including 'Decline of the English Murder' (*Tribune*), 'Politics and the English Language' (*Horizon*), 'Why I Write' (*Gangrel*), 'Politics vs. Literature' (*Polemic*). Working on his novel in increasingly poor health.

1947 Writes his last 'As I Please' column for *Tribune* in April. Independence for India and Pakistan, August. Most of the year spent in Jura, writing *Nineteen Eighty-Four*. 'Such, Such Were the Joys' drafted.

1948 The first half of the year spent in hospital in East Kilbride, near Glasgow, with tuberculosis of the left lung. The rest of the year spent in Jura, where *Nineteen Eighty-Four* is completed in December, and followed by a serious relapse in health.

1949 Very ill with tuberculosis in Cotswold Sanatorium at Cranham, Gloucestershire, and from September in University College Hospital, London. *Nineteen Eighty-Four* published by Secker & Warburg in June.

	Marriage to Sonia Bronwell in October, in University College Hospital.
1950	George Orwell dies of pulmonary tuberculosis, 26 January, and is buried in Sutton Courtenay, Oxfordshire. By the end of the year, *Nineteen Eighty-Four* has been published in Danish, Japanese, Swedish, German, Dutch, French, Norwegian, Finnish, Italian, and Hebrew, and *Animal Farm* in Portuguese, Swedish, Norwegian, German, Polish, Persian, Dutch, French, Italian, Gujarati, Ukrainian, Danish, Estonian, Spanish, Korean, Japanese, Telugu, Indonesian, Icelandic, and Russian editions.

Abbreviations

AF	*Animal Farm*, ed. Peter Davison (Harmondsworth: Penguin, 1989)
BD	*Burmese Days*, ed. Peter Davison (Harmondsworth: Penguin, 1989)
CD	*A Clergyman's Daughter*, ed. Peter Davison (Harmondsworth: Penguin, 1990)
CUA	*Coming Up for Air*, ed. Peter Davison (Harmondsworth: Penguin, 2001)
CW	*The Complete Works of George Orwell*, ed. Peter Davison, 20 vols. (London: Secker & Warburg, 1998)
D&O	*Down and Out in Paris and London*, ed. Peter Davison (Harmondsworth: Penguin, 2001)
HC	*Homage to Catalonia*, ed. Peter Davison (Harmondsworth: Penguin, 1989)
KAF	*Keep the Aspidistra Flying*, ed. Peter Davison (Harmondsworth: Penguin, 1989)
NEF	*Nineteen Eighty-Four*, ed. Peter Davison (Harmondsworth: Penguin, 1989)
RWP	*The Road to Wigan Pier*, ed. Peter Davison (Harmondsworth: Penguin, 1989)

Page references in the text, such as (*CUA* 23), are to the Penguin editions, whose pagination corresponds to the first nine volumes of *CW*.

1

Introduction

Eric Blair stood out. From his early teenage years he was unusually tall, and in his twenties he became thin and gaunt. From photographs in which he stands with other people he stares out uncomfortably, a gangling figure built to a different scale, a one-man awkward squad. His feeling of conspicuous incongruity went back to his childhood, when he was sure he was ugly and unlovable; but it was also lifelong, and not simply a matter of appearance. He spoke English in an accent, formed in Henley-on-Thames and polished at Eton, that marked him as a member of a class widely and, he felt, justifiably resented by most ordinary people. It was unmistakable, and inescapable. As he lay dying at Cranham in 1949, he heard it in the 'upper-class English voices' of some visitors to the hospital. 'No wonder everyone hates us so' (*CW* xx. 92), he wrote in his diary. Yet he was not simply 'upper class'. He belonged, by his own meticulous description, to the lower upper-middle class, a precarious and unrewarding status that often seemed to make him uncomfortable with the social categories both above and below. The insecure scholarship boy at preparatory school and then at Eton went on to serve as a police officer among the often restive and sometimes openly hostile Burmese. There he found himself an increasingly compromised member of the colonial *sahiblog*, a caste convinced of their natural and cultural superiority over the subject people, though most of them, he observed, would not pass as gentlemen back in the home country.

He returned from the colonial East, which had become intolerable to him, to an England where he felt he did not belong, and was soon finding new forms of awkwardness – the genteel down and out who solicited and recorded the life stories of tramps he met on the road, but told them lies about his own; the bohemian radical, washing dishes in the filthy sculleries of a luxury Parisian hotel. When he finished his first book, his identity as a writer seemed to fit so clumsily to his former or other self that he seriously considered publishing under the pseudonym of 'X', before deciding on 'George Orwell' at the last minute. Orwell's autobiographical writing is full of images of an incongruity that is sometimes ludicrous but could also be painful and even dangerous. We see him as the gangling intellectual, bent almost double and stumbling along miles of tunnel in a northern coal mine, or the tall foreigner picked out by a sniper in the trenches of Aragón, fighting in someone else's civil war. Intellectually he was a displaced person, who struggled to unlearn the ideological reflexes that came with his upbringing, but was never at home in any orthodoxy. For the last dozen years of his life he was committed to the socialist cause, but was also one of its most unwelcome critics. Many socialists distrusted him and some despised him. Sometimes he distrusted and despised himself. He was an internationalist and an English patriot, an anti-imperialist who broadcast propaganda to India urging loyalty to the British Empire. He lived in dozens of places and stayed nowhere for long. He did not belong. This singular inability to fit in was not a source of romantic self-satisfaction to him, but it was a fact of life. It guaranteed his unorthodoxy (he was a man who would have been orthodox if he could), giving him a humanistic insight into the speciality of all cases, and a sensitivity to the often abrasive interactions of person and place, subject and context, individual and collective.

This study of Orwell's writing approaches it in terms of a series of contexts, each context being a place on the map but also a field of themes and problems, a contestation. The chapter on the East introduces the issues of empire, authority, and justice that Orwell encountered there, a cluster of ideas that, in its various mutations, was to remain his capital subject. It also opens up questions of complicity and dissent – and the uncomfortable place of the dissident under authority who is also its agent and beneficiary – that travel right through to *Nineteen Eighty-Four*. This chapter foregrounds *Burmese Days*, the Burma essays, and the BBC work. It was in a colonial context that Orwell's ideas of England and what it could mean began to take shape (his writing is postcolonial), and England is the subject of the second chapter, which examines principally his three novels of English life, the documentary *The Road to Wigan Pier*, and some of the journalism. The chief themes here are class, culture, and language, and in particular the way Orwell saw England as the site of a shifting but ceaseless struggle between warring discourses – of classes, institutions, ideologies – in which he and his heroes (and heroine) are more or less unwillingly conscripted. The chapter on Europe deals with war and revolution, from *Homage to Catalonia* to *Animal Farm*, and some of Orwell's less well-known writing on wartime and post-war Europe. The aspiring young English writer was drawn to Paris in 1928, and the newly politically conscious author was drawn to Spain in 1936. Europe could be a place for escape, solidarity, resistance; its ideological battleground soon became a literal one. In continental Europe in the age of the dictators, the Englishman might be a cosmopolitan, a tourist, a reporter, a comrade, an enemy, a fugitive; he was always both a European and a foreigner. In 1945 Orwell was travelling across a ruined Germany, looking for the signs of what a post-war Europe might come to mean, and contemplating a novel to be entitled *The Last Man in Europe*. My final chapter concentrates on Orwell's first completely imaginary fictional context, the future Oceania of *Nineteen Eighty-Four*. Here again, rather than the relation between persons, the main subject of the novel is the person in place (and out of place), the individual in the context of a geography, politics, ideology, and language. Winston Smith is placed in a mimetic space uncompromised by its author's complex history of dislocations. But this nowhere, this warped utopia, is furnished with the imagery, and haunted by the preoccupations, of Orwell's empire, England, and Europe.

It is not surprising that the awkwardness that characterized his life and writing should manifest itself in an ambivalence and indecision about writing itself. The self-contradictory moves of his 1946 essay 'Why I Write' (*CW* xviii. 316–21) are part of an unfinished argument Orwell carried on with himself on this subject. He belonged to a generation that had learned from Freud to look for the origins of behaviour and disposition in the individual's early history, and he gives his opinion that his career as a writer has its origins in childhood loneliness and low self-esteem, and its motive in compensation for his early feelings of failure in everyday life. Of the four kinds of reasons for which people write – egoistic, aesthetic, historical, and political – he declares that in his case the first three would 'by nature' outweigh the last. But something appears to have gone wrong. He finds himself trapped in an uncongenial sort of writing – 'forced into becoming a sort of pamphleteer' – and throughout the previous ten years all his ambitions have focused on a kind of work in which private motivations and aesthetic pleasures can be seen only as irrelevant and frivolous. There must be a constant struggle to efface the personality; and style too must be mortified, for 'good prose is like a windowpane', clear, undecorated, invisibly drawing the attention through itself to the object on the other side. But Orwell's recourse to figurative language ('like a windowpane') to make the point memorably also serves to contradict it. And his Protestant-sounding distrust of rhetoric and personality is subverted by his romantic admission that writing is driven by an 'emotional attitude' formed in early life, so that, for a writer, to escape these early influences would be to kill the impulse to write. Further, he acknowledges that he himself would not be able to do the work of writing if it were not also an aesthetic experience. Still, it is invariably where he lacks a political purpose, he thinks, that his writing becomes pompous, overdecorated, and lifeless. And so on.

'Why I Write' is ungainly, full of the language of effort and strain ('It can be seen how these various impulses must war against one another'), and its author sees his writing as struggling towards forms of reconciliation – such as his wish 'to make political writing into an art' – without ever quite arriving there; his next book 'is bound to be a failure', but then 'every book is a failure', an admission that brings him back to the still unappeased feelings of childhood inadequacy from which he set out. The writing, early or late, undertaken in the first place to deal with an unhappy dislocation between subject and environment (to refashion the subject psychologically, or to change the place politically) ends up reproducing that dislocation, replacing it in the writing itself. It becomes formalized, in his uncertainty, especially in his early writing, as to how close to stand to his main characters (including his autobiographical selves), and in an unsureness about the kind of response he wants from his readers, an unsureness perhaps exemplified by his generic explorations in the frontier territory between fiction and non-fiction, and between literary writing and journalism. But above all it is thematized, in a series of narratives about displacement and disappointment and defeat, a failure of Orwell's people – and of course of his animals – to be able or permitted to live in the kind of place in which they could feel they belonged. In the age of the displaced person, this makes Orwell seem, perhaps more than anyone else, a writer of his time. In dramatizing and communicating exclusion, unease, and isolation, his work creates paradoxically a kind of solidarity. And his bleakest stories about the triumphs of injustice and inhumanity are predicated on a humanist belief in the right to justice, which they passionately reinforce.

2

East

In October 1922 when Eric Blair boarded the liner that was to take him from Liverpool to Rangoon, he was embarking on independent adult life. The East was a career, a field of action, and a test. He was 19. His boyhood had been privileged, rather lonely, and entirely predictable – five years as a boarding pupil at preparatory school, a term at Wellington, and four and a half years at Eton, punctuated by holidays with his provincial and rather staid middle-class family. He had been born in India, in Bengal, but returned with his mother to England when he was a year old and had hardly ever since been abroad. Now he was leaving to start a career in the Indian Imperial Police in Burma. Though he might have been expected to go first to university, his journey to the East was itself part of a familiar pattern. His parents had met in India and both their families had a history of involvement in the Orient. His mother grew up in Moulmein, in Lower Burma, where her family were in the teak trade. His father, who belonged to the administrative middle class that supplied the managers and officers of the British Empire, had retired ten years earlier, in 1912, from the Indian Civil Service. In India he had spent his whole career in the Opium Department, which was responsible for maintaining the highest standards of purity in the drug whose sale was still a lucrative monopoly of the government of British India. Coming from a family of the military and imperial class, and a country recently emerged from a long war in France and Flanders, the young man boarding the P&O liner in 1922 would never quite shake off the sense that England was a place where nothing much ever happened. The action was elsewhere, and he was leaving home to find it.

He spent five years in the police in colonial Burma. Both family tradition and education had prepared him for service in the empire. Pay in the imperial police was good, and a young Englishman in the East could enjoy a prestige and lifestyle superior to anything he could have expected at home. But this was a difficult time to be a policeman in British Burma. There was the usual level of crime to punish or prevent, and there were inter-ethnic sensibilities to deal with. But, in addition to this, there was throughout the 1920s an underlying feeling of discontent, sometimes surfacing in forms of civil disorder. Many Burmese were angry not to have benefited more, and more quickly, from the kind of localizing reforms the British had started introducing in India after the First World War, and the nationalist movement in India, demanding an end to British rule, was finding an echo in neighbouring Burma. The Burmese resented the British, and the British resented their unpopularity. All George Orwell's writing about Burma testifies to a highly strung atmosphere of suspicion, sometimes unconcealed hostility, and mutual incomprehension. It was an unhappy country. The 24-year-old police inspector returned to Europe in July 1927, and soon afterwards he resigned his commission in the imperial police. He never returned to the East. By the end of his five years in Burma, he said later, 'I hated the imperialism I was serving with a bitterness which I probably cannot make clear' (*RWP* 134). But this is only part of the story. He resigned not only because he no longer wanted to be an imperial policeman, but also because he was determined to be a writer. His first published novel, *Burmese Days*, was about the East. So was his last project in fiction, 'A Smoking-Room Story' (*CW* xx. 188–200), which he set aside when he became too ill to write. And there are other ways in which the East, and how it might be represented, was the theme of his whole writing career.

The problem of representation has two dimensions, of what is to be seen, and of where you stand to observe it. These related questions, of topic and modality, are broached in quite complex ways in the simple story 'A Hanging' (*CW* x. 207–10), published over the name of Eric A. Blair in the *Adelphi* in 1931, three years before *Burmese Days*. For a start, it is unclear whether the narrative is offered as fact or fiction. Orwell said he had attended a hanging in Burma (*RWP* 136–7), but this would not have been part of his official police duties and there is no proof that he did – or, of course, if he did, whether this story is or purports to be an accurate account of the experience. The European narrator of the story does not seem to have any part to play in the proceedings and it is never quite clear what he is doing there; he is an underdetermined blur in the middle of the picture. The scene in the prison yard, when the condemned man is escorted to his execution, is set with an impersonal and quite fussy attention to detail and procedure. This includes taking a measure of cultural distances, for, although the Europeans present are not identified as such until the last paragraph, all the Asians are ethnically labelled – the Hindu prisoner, Eurasian jailer, Burmese magistrate, and so on. Orientals are also distanced from a European norm by the deviances of their quaint and pompous speech from the style of the narrative discourse, and the condemned man himself – barely human in appearance, a 'puny wisp of a man' – is further estranged by the detail of his moustache, which makes him look unreal, like 'a comic man on the films'. All of this seems designed to emphasize the difference between the narrator and the natives, the European colonial observer and the Eastern scene.

Then comes a moment that we will come to recognize as a characteristically Orwellian epiphany. From nowhere a dog appears. 'Wild with glee at finding so many human beings together,' it capers about, and jumps up to try to lick the prisoner's face. In that moment, the careful ritual of the execution is disrupted, and one consequence is that the narrator suddenly and for a moment sees everything differently. From his point of view, identified as he is with colonial penal authority, the occasion can be justified and coherent only if it rests on an extreme distance, a radical difference, between himself and the condemned man, and between himself and the oriental functionaries doing (as Orwell called it elsewhere) the dirty work of empire. But the dog had looked at the procession with an eye blind to hierarchy, difference, innocence, or guilt, and had seen simply 'many human beings together'. Now, when the narrator looks again at the prisoner, as he steps slightly aside to avoid a puddle, for a moment he sees as it were through the skin, through the ethnic difference, to recognize the other as a man like himself. The prisoner's body, still busy to the last at its secret physiological functions (food digesting, nails growing), is now seen as a sign not of difference but of kinship; for a moment the execution is revealed as a fratricide, the original crime of violence. The condemned man and his executioners are in the same order of nature. 'He and we were a party of men walking together,' as the dog's innocent vision had seen immediately. It is a simple revelation that illuminates not only the issue of capital punishment, but also the conditions of ethnicity and empire in which that punishment is to be performed. 'When a murderer is hanged,' Orwell wrote during his last illness, 'there is only one person present at the ceremony who is not guilty of murder. . . . Everyone who has ever seen an execution knows this' (*CW* xx. 213).

It is an essential part of the meaning of this oriental epiphany that it has no effect on what happens. The execution proceeds. 'There was a clanking noise, and then dead silence. The prisoner had vanished, and the rope was twisting on itself.' The narrator, burdened by the awkward insight that he has immediately had to smother, joins the other white men and their good native subordinates for a drink, with much semi-hysterical joking. 'The dead man was a hundred yards away.'

The pattern here is worth dwelling on for a moment, because we will find it again in Orwell's writings East and West. First there is a phase of estrangement, a measurement of distance, perhaps even a feeling of revulsion, as the observer approaches his subject with a sense of his own natural difference and superiority. The other is perceived as being of a lower order, irredeemably alien, instinctual, mindless, either dangerous or pathetic. But then, through some shift of viewpoint, the object of observation is seen to be inhabited by an independent inner life and integrity, and makes a claim on the observer that he can no longer ignore; they belong after all together. But to glimpse a relationship or kinship with the other is inevitably then to be reminded of how that kinship has been violated, betrayed, and lost. And so, in a third phase, a sort of crisis of insufficiency and guilt turns the observer's gaze back upon himself. This is the point at which the narrator observes himself at the end of the story, shamefacedly drinking and laughing with the executioners, for after all his place is among them; he cannot deny that is why he is there in the first place. Much of what is characteristic in Orwell's later writing has this same awkward modality, making shift with a spatially and politically compromised point of view, and an uncomfortable fit between the observer and the scene. It was in the East that these manœuvres began.

This awkward, lurching modality applied to Orwell's orientation to place as well as to people. He writes a lot about the natural world and landscape of the East, and about its animal life. The landscapes of Burma, he said, so haunted him that he was obliged to write a novel about them to get rid of them (*RWP* 101), and yet it was not just the memory of the landscape that *Burmese Days* attempted to exorcise. Several years later, on a prolonged visit to French colonial Morocco, he made a discovery about his own observations that he was ready to generalize, in the essay 'Marrakech': in a hot country, anywhere south of Gibraltar or east of Suez, it was easier to notice the natural world than to see the inhabitants. 'In a tropical landscape one's eye takes in everything except the human beings,' he noticed. 'People with brown skins are next door to invisible' (*CW* x. 418, 420). All colonial empires were founded, he suggested, on this half-admitted disbelief in the humanity of the colonized population. The colonial gaze is distracted from the human to the animal life and landscape of the other place (a distraction often confirmed by European explorers' claims to 'discover' places in the earth already perfectly well known to the people who lived there, and their tendency to write and behave as if lands new to them were unpopulated). This attention to the natural world might be read as a trope that dehumanizes the oriental space so as to justify control and domination of it. But in Orwell's writing about the East, it does not work. As with the initial dehumanizing of the condemned man in 'A Hanging', a disregarded and denied human truth asserts itself after all, abolishing both the distance and the hierarchy that separate and protect the colonial observer and set him both above and apart from what is in front of him. Observing the natural world may be a way of not noticing the human one, but in Orwell's writing the human always comes back, like the Burmese faces he said haunted his dreams (*RWP* 138); and in dreams, as Yeats says, begins responsibility.

The most famous example is the story 'Shooting an Elephant' (*CW* x. 501–6), written in 1936, after *Burmese Days*. There the pattern is identical to 'A Hanging'. The English observer finds himself, because of who he is, obliged to kill an elephant, which has gone out of control, destroyed property, and trampled a coolie to death. This is not a wild beast, but a working elephant that has broken free and become destructive, so the English policeman is not engaged in the equivalent of a civilizing mission, but is bent on crushing a mutiny, and also – since a large native crowd has gathered – on a demonstration of power. He approaches the great beast in the extreme of estrangement: it is a killer, and he carries a murderous weapon. When he gets close to the animal, however, it is peacefully eating grass in a field, obviously no longer dangerous, and, says the policeman narrator, 'I knew with perfect certainty that I ought not to shoot him.' The shift of pronoun – the moment it comes into sight, the animal is no longer 'it' but 'he' – corresponds to the humanizing moment of intimacy on the execution ground in 'A Hanging', when the criminal mutely claimed kin with the man who was going to help to kill him. But in both cases, the awkward epiphany is not powerful enough to stop the process. The sight of the peaceful elephant brings a realization of an essentially innocent oneness between the human and the natural world. Appropriate enough in a Buddhist country like Burma, for Orwell and his English readers it is also an idea that has a whole tradition of romantic writing behind it. But this natural piety is overridden by a stronger imperative, that of the discourse of colonialism and the policeman's part in it; once again, he has to remind himself why he is there. His prestige is at stake. Surrounded by an immense crowd, the white man with the gun has to perform his fixed role in the theatre of empire, and do his duty and kill the beast, even though he now recognizes that 'it would be murder to shoot him'. The human pronoun is now reinforced by the scandalous naming of the act as murder, which assumes a human perpetrator and victim. 'A sahib has got to act like a sahib,' which now means it is his job to commit murder. It is another case in which a relation between the European and the non-human world ends up revealing an uncomfortable truth: natural history recapitulates colonial history.

It gets worse, of course, when the elephant is shot but does not die. The policeman is forced to go up to the stricken beast, and he stares 'far down into caverns of pale pink throat'. As with the condemned man, an insight – literal in this case – into the elephant's interiority makes his killing more unforgivable. The policeman has to pour shot after shot into his heart and down his throat. By the end of the story the narrator returns guiltily, as he did in 'A Hanging', to the company of his own people. He is alienated not only from the place, and the natural world, but also from himself, for he has betrayed himself, and done violence not only to the elephant but also to his own romantic insight. Some Europeans tell him he was right to shoot the elephant, others say it was a shame to shoot it just because it killed a coolie, since the animal was worth much more than the man. His last thought is that he is glad that the coolie was killed, because this has put him legally in the right and given him a sufficient pretext for shooting the elephant. British imperialism was always tangled up with sport and particularly hunting, and its literature and folk memory are full of adventurous tales of the encounter between man and beast. But this animal story is about brutalization. The narrator shows how, being obliged to uphold colonial prestige, he has revealed himself to be the sort of man he despises. It is a revelation, even so, inseparable from the self-pity of his axiom that 'when the white man turns tyrant it is his own freedom that he destroys'. This sounds very like the voice of John Flory, the central character of the novel *Burmese Days* (1934).

In the novel, the colonial presence is registered on the landscape of Burma as a series of bursts of clarity – the dazzling white bungalows, the white-walled cemetery, the 'spiritual citadel' of the Club – standing out against the dull and indistinct background of khaki-coloured maidan, ochreous river, and native town hidden in green groves of trees. This is Kyauktada, an upcountry backwater with some 4,000 inhabitants, where Flory is one of seven Europeans clinging to a rock of tawdry European culture. There is a kind of war between European civilization and Burmese nature and culture, and there seems to be a misfit between the colonial map and the

Burmese territory. If the British have their way, Flory cynically tells his friend Dr Veraswami, in due course Burma's forests, villages, monasteries, and pagodas will all have disappeared, to be replaced with a replica suburban England, of pink villas fifty yards apart – 'all over those hills, as far as you can see, villa after villa, with all the gramophones playing the same tune' (*BD* 40). From their legal system to their railway terminus, the British have imposed a grid of colonial discipline on a sluggish and unruly landscape, which nonetheless is always threatening to overwhelm its new masters, just as in the garden of the Club, on the edge of the jungle, nature seems to retaliate against the invader, causing the English flowers neatly planted there to overflow their borders in a riot of vast size and richness. Even the light is an enemy. 'Bloody, bloody hole!' are Flory's first words in the novel (*BD* 15), as he steps out of the joyless sanctuary of his house into the merciless glare of Burmese day. The Europeans hate Kyauktada, and to them the jungle in particular is unfriendly, an alien and unruly place of discomfort and danger. A rebellion will be fomented in the jungle, Maxwell the Forest Officer is murdered there, and Lackersteen, a suburban Mr Kurtz, goes to the dogs in the forest unsupervised by his shrewish wife.

But what singles Flory out from all the other Europeans is his feelings for the natural world, which become clear when he goes for one of his habitual walks with his dog into the jungle, in the fourth chapter. The edge or surface of the forest that he broaches is ugly and unwelcoming, dried up and lifeless. But as he moves alone into the interior, along a track few human beings and no other Europeans ever follow, a different Burma appears to him, a place not of hostility but of beauty and benediction. He comes to a clear pool beneath a peepul tree, where he strips and steps into the water. Unarmed, unclothed, and unmoving, in a state of trusting vulnerability that is as close as he can come to innocence, he lies in the water, watching the doves in the branches above him. Time stops; and for once in his clumsy life it is natural for Flory to be where he is, as integral a part of a scene of nature as the birds whose colour matches the leaves. He seems for a moment of stillness to be as perfectly adapted as they are to the environment of which tree, water, birds, and man together are the constituents. With its distinctly Wordsworthian overtones, this sylvan moment under 'the great green dome of the tree' (*BD* 56–7) naturalizes Flory's presence in Burma, so that he belongs, as long as it lasts, in an unantagonistic relation between Western subject and Eastern place. It is a poignant moment because it depends on his forgetting (or escaping from) the colonial present and his own part as an agent, beneficiary, and victim of colonial history. But time resumes, and with it Flory's unhappiness; history replaces natural history, Flory remembers why he is there and that there is no one with whom he can share the beauty of the scene. 'Alone, alone, the bitterness of being alone!' (*BD* 57).

However hedonistic and unproprietorial his instincts may be, Flory is an Englishman in colonial Burma. He is not his own man. Things are expected of him. He is reminded of where his loyalties should lie every time he steps into the European Club at Kyauktada, which is every day, since there is nowhere else to go. But most of all it is the arrival of the beautiful Elizabeth Lackersteen, fresh from England, that brings home to Flory what is expected of an Englishman in the East. At their first meeting, Flory earns her admiration by romantically rescuing her from an entirely harmless buffalo. If Burmese nature for Flory is Rousseauesque and kindly, Elizabeth sees it as Hobbesian and beastly. She has brought to Burma a quasi-paranoid theory of natural history, and colonial history, so that she assumes humankind and nature to be forever at war, just as she assumes the relationship between West and East, British and Burmese, to be always one of antagonism. She takes it for granted that the buffalo wants to kill her. Looking at the Burmese people around her, she declares that their skulls are of a shape that, she has read in a magazine somewhere, indicates a criminal type (*BD* 122).

All this is nonsense to Flory, who nonetheless has fallen hopelessly in love with Elizabeth, and realizes that to win her he must be the sort of man she admires. At the same time he is under pressure from the other Europeans at the Club, which comprises his entire social world, to show some ethnic solidarity with them in their embattled determination to keep their distance from, and above, the Burmese who surround and hugely outnumber them. And so Flory finds himself, against his better instincts, pressed into playing the conventional role of the Englishman in the colonial orient. To impress Elizabeth, he takes her into the jungle, not for a harmless nature walk, but for a hunting trip in which he teaches her to slaughter those emblematically pacific doves we saw him admiring earlier at the jungle pool. When a leopard turns up, they kill it; Flory wants to give her the leopard's skin. This is orthodox, in the cultural context; it is the sort of thing men do and women expect. For Elizabeth's benefit, the harmless swimmer and wanderer of the earlier chapter now performs the part of the white hunter, casting himself as a sporting predator and reducing the jungle to an emporium of potential trophies. He surrenders, in other words, to a strong colonial discourse, and allows the established idiom of imperialist behaviour to carry him along like a tide. The role takes him over, as it was to do for the policeman facing the elephant; he becomes a stereotype. Flory conforms to a pre-existing matrix and becomes what Elizabeth all along expected him to be. In doing so he confirms her prejudices – that Burma, and wild nature, are both dangerous and barbarically different, and are there to be triumphed over and controlled; that to be a European is to hold a natural sovereignty over the East; and that to be human, and especially to be manly, is to stand above and dominate the natural world. Flory entirely betrays his own weak liberal sentiments, in the pattern of 'A Hanging' and 'Shooting an Elephant', to buy a place among his own people whom he despises. The consequent self-loathing, at the end of the story, expresses itself in his suicide, but only after he has confirmed his apostasy from natural piety by first turning the gun on his faithful dog, Flo, and blowing her brains out.

Flory in fact has equally tortuous relations both with Burma and with the version of England embodied in the Club; he is alternately revolted and fascinated, aloof and immersed, supplicating and excluded. After fifteen years working as a timber merchant in Burma, he is spoilt for England, but recognizes the Empire as 'a despotism with theft as its final object' (*BD* 68), and is fully aware of his own complicity in it; he keeps to himself this loss of faith in empire, at the cost of his self-respect. So he is a conformist and a secret dissident, his sense of isolation and self-hatred increasing from year to year, for 'it is a corrupting thing to live one's real life in secret' (*BD* 70). Undoubtedly Orwell knew what this state of mind was like, and indeed in *The Road to Wigan Pier* he was to suggest that all over India there were Englishmen who secretly loathed the empire they were part of. Although Flory is not Orwell's self-portrait, there are mawkish moments in the novel when the narrative seems virtually to identify itself with Flory ('Alone, alone, the bitterness of being alone!'), perhaps traces of the story's beginning in the form of a first-personal narrative, of which some drafts survive (*CW* x. 93–104).

The truth was, Orwell believed, that, though it might be benevolent and even necessary, British rule in the East was an unjustifiable and atavistic tyranny. 'No modern man, in his heart of hearts, believes that it is right to invade a foreign country and hold the population down by force' (*RWP* 135). He was to remember that the very first thing he saw on arrival in the East, as the ship docked in Colombo, was a white police sergeant kicking a coolie (*CW* xii. 121). It was a thing, he said, that simply could not have happened in Paddington station in London, or the Liverpool docks: the policeman would not dare, and, if he did, the porter would retaliate. We might add, though Orwell does not, that it could not have happened in the 'white' empire, in Sydney or Nova Scotia. What made it a routine sight in the East was a pervasive racism, the assumption that Asians, and Africans, were less fully human than white people. (In conversation in the Club at Kyauktada, Ellis refers to Burmese as 'niggers', though Macgregor mildly demurs.) This ideology of categorical difference, and the institutions and behaviours and beliefs that rested on it, is the main political theme of *Burmese Days*. It was vivid, dramatic, and inescapable in the East, since there it was visible, as it were, in colour. But it was to remain Orwell's central political preoccupation. Injustice followed from a disbelief in equality. The lesson that was to be inscribed on the barn wall at Animal Farm had been learned in the colonial East, where some human beings were more human than others.

The European Club is at the centre of Kyauktada, and at the centre of the novel's plot, which revolves around the question of who belongs and who does not. Every European is automatically a member, but the Kyauktada club is one of the last in Burma to exclude all local people, and now Macgregor, the Deputy Commissioner, has proposed that they elect an oriental to membership. The proposal precipitates a crisis of difference, a form of identity crisis, among the members of the Club, most of whom are fiercely opposed to the idea. Even a 'good native' member, entering their space and sharing their status, seems an intolerable threat to what they think themselves to be. Though the Club is flyblown and depressing and it is hard to imagine anyone wanting to join it, the question is of great symbolic importance because of the prestige that would attach to a local who became a member. The two likely candidates are the Indian Dr Veraswami, Flory's friend and an enthusiastic Anglophile, and the clever and corrupt U Po Kyin, the Burmese divisional magistrate. U Po Kyin's successful campaign to discredit Veraswami and Flory balances Flory's wooing of Elizabeth in a way that makes this the best plotted of Orwell's novels.

The English in *Burmese Days* are dreadful, and bring to mind Orwell's opinion that there was not much good English writing about the East because no one capable of describing the atmosphere could bear to stay there long enough to do so (*CW* x. 508). (He made exceptions of Forster's *A Passage to India* and the fiction of Conrad and Somerset Maugham; as for Kipling, he wrote in 1936, 'I worshipped [him] at thirteen, loathed him at seventeen, enjoyed him at twenty, despised him at twenty-five and now again rather admire him' (*CW* x. 409).) The European world of Kyauktada is recognizably Kipling's world, but without any of the glamour, heroism, humour, or zest. Its inhabitants – the drunk Lackersteen and his bossy wife, the pathologically racist Ellis, the mediocre Macgregor – are the literary descendants of the colonial personnel Kipling had so admired, but now out of sorts, peevish, and defensive as they feel British authority and prestige beginning to weaken in the East after the First World War, the groundswell of nationalism in India, and the Amritsar massacre. They are bigoted and philistine. Their chief cultural activity, apart from drinking, is gossip, and they are obsessively jealous of their privileges. Their main aim in life seems to be to perpetuate the way of life they enjoy (though that is not the right word), and the political and racial inequality that supports it. In themselves, the British in the East might be 'dull, decent people' (*BD* 69), of a harmless suburban cast, but when encouraged to think of themselves as the *sahiblog*, a master race governing and served by a whole people inferior to themselves, they can scarcely avoid becoming overbearing and unjust. They are the prisoners of their own fantasy of superiority, their dreary talk at the Club going round and round, recycling the myths and slogans of their own racial prestige. 'Was it possible', thinks Flory, 'that they could go on week after week, year after year, repeating word for word the same evil-minded drivel, like a parody of a fifth-rate story in *Blackwood's*?' (*BD* 31). But this is their world, and it is an early instance in Orwell of the power of a discourse to determine how reality is experienced.

Other people in Burma relate to it too. Dr Veraswami, in his habitual debates with Flory about the Empire, is an auto-orientalist. He holds unswervingly to the line that the British are the selfless purveyors of education, progress, and modernity, vouchsafed to undeserving people like himself, handicapped by the superstition and apathy of the oriental character. The two derelict Eurasians, Francis and Samuel, speak a sort of comic-*babu* English and insist desperately on the difference between the 'natives' and 'us'. Flory's Burmese mistress, Ma Hla May, probably has few illusions about the British character, but she is enthralled by the prestige she enjoys as a *bo-kadaw*, a white man's wife. When Flory rejects her, after the arrival on the scene of Elizabeth Lackersteen, Ma Hla May is reduced to nothing, for she cannot return to her village. When she begs him abjectly to take her back, in the most powerful and distressing scene in the novel (*BD* 157–62), Flory can see how completely he has despoiled and corrupted her. Even the villainous U Po Kyin, who understands enough about the British to be able to outwit them easily, is a creature of the same discourse of empire. His whole life, since his earliest memory of the British troops marching into Mandalay back in the 1880s, has been a brilliant exploitation of colonial institutions and states of mind. He despises his own people, and hatches his plots not for money or even power (he already has plenty of both) but for the prestige of association with the British. He controls the political life of the Burmese in Kyauktada, but, far from being subversive, his activities are contained within the matrix of the colonial status system. The discourse of nationalism in the novel is shown to offer no effective resistance to that of empire. Burmese nationalist activity, as U Po Kyin manipulates it, is sometimes noisy but always in the end futile. Nothing changes except individual prestige – Po Kyin up, Verswami down, Flory out.

Orwell seems by his own account to have returned to Europe possessed by a kind of self-hatred, nursed in solitude and secret during his years in Burma, a double reaction against empire and against his own professional participation in its dirty work. There is something ungainly and perhaps naive about his subsequent experiments in dispossession, those acts of exorcism or expiation he describes in the English part of *Down and Out in Paris and London*. His adventures among the homeless were, as he admits, a masquerade (*RWP* 140), and it was not really any more possible to 'go native' in England, or Paris, than it would have been in Moulmein. Going on the road as a tramp was a gesture as compromised in its way as those romantic but futile intimations of kinship that interrupted proceedings in 'A Hanging' and 'Shooting a Elephant'. But, gesture though it was, faintly ridiculous though it may have been ('I am a difficult person to disguise, being abnormally tall' (*RWP* 140)), it was a protest against inequality. And although that meaning was, at the time, an entirely private one, it set off a train of action that most of Orwell's published writing was to continue. It made another statement, too, on which the rest of his career would be an elaboration. The East was connected to the West. Injustice was indivisible. 'And what should they know of England who only England know?', Kipling had asked rhetorically, and Orwell agreed. Although his own political position was not particularly coherent in 1927 when he came back from Burma, he never thought in terms of 'only England'; the nation was possessed of an empire, and the injustice to be found in Whitechapel or Wigan was inseparable from that to be found in Mandalay, though one expressed itself in terms of class and the other in terms of race.

In radical mood after his return from Spain in 1937, he declared that it was futile to be anti-Fascist while attempting to preserve capitalism, not to mention its off-shoot imperialism – British rule in India, for instance, being 'just as bad' as

German Fascism (*CW* xi. 80). Still, a description of Orwell as anti-imperialist needs some qualification, especially after the outbreak of the Second World War in 1939. 'If I thought a victory in the present war would mean nothing beyond a new lease of life for British imperialism,' he wrote truculently during the 'phoney war' in the spring of 1940, 'I should be inclined to side with Russia and Germany' (*CW* xii. 122–3). But later that year Britain itself was threatened with invasion, and in late 1941 Japan entered the war, and soon swept through Britain's imperial possessions in south-east Asia, overran Burma, and was poised to attack India. By this time Orwell was working as a Talks Assistant, later Talks Producer, in the Indian Section of the Eastern Service of the British Broadcasting Corporation (BBC). Though it was a publicly funded corporation and not a government department, nobody seriously believed or argued that in wartime the BBC would be independent of the government, least of all in its overseas services. The British Government's policy on India, and the rest of the Empire, was that its continued loyalty was essential to winning the war. Why did Orwell the anti-imperialist, whose *Burmese Days* was still banned in India, take part willingly in broadcasts to the East whose purpose was to secure the loyalty of Indians to the British Empire at war?

He wrote and produced cultural and educational programmes for the Eastern Service, but his main propaganda work was in a series of weekly news reviews broadcast to India, Malaya, and Indonesia, discussing and interpreting for his listeners the events in the war around the world. As Japanese forces moved closer to the Indian border, the British were increasingly nervous about the loyalty of their Indian subjects. In 1942 Gandhi and the Congress leaders had been imprisoned, after refusing to suspend their agitation for Indian independence until the Japanese threat should be over. Privately Orwell profoundly disagreed with these detentions. Nevertheless, in his news reviews he does put forward the argument that at this critical time India's interests, and survival, coincide with those of its imperial masters. His position is that an end to British rule in India is desirable, and inevitable, in the longer term, but its continuation is desirable, and essential for India's protection, in the immediate term (the classic argument of liberal imperialism for more than a century). He directly confronts Japanese propaganda aimed at India that claimed that the Japanese were bent on liberating Asia from its white colonial masters, by pointing to Japanese imperialist encroachments in China and elsewhere, and citing the racism of Japanese official discourse; in the circumstances, he points out, siding with the British was a refuge for India against a more aggressive imperialism from the East. For his Indian listeners he interprets the war not as an imperialist struggle, of course (except on the part of the Japanese), but a global conflict in which all peoples have a stake. He frequently asks them to imagine a map of the globe, in which the war is taking its course all over the world as 'the struggle of free peoples who see before them the chance of a fuller and happier existence, against comparatively small cliques who are not interested in the general development of humanity but only in advancing their individual power' (*CW* xiii. 324). In a world war, freedom was indivisible. Like it or not, he went on, 'India is already in the struggle; and the outcome of the war – and therefore India's independence – may be determined to a very great extent by the efforts that Indians themselves now make'.

The last part of the argument was crucial. India would have a better chance of independence if the British and the Allies, not the Japanese and the Axis, won the war. At this moment, in early 1942 under the threat of invasion, India was the centre of the war, and therefore the centre of the world (*CW* xiii. 180), and the outcome of the war was in India's hands. The Allied cause was India's to lose, and with it India's future as a postcolonial nation. If it resisted, shoulder to shoulder with the British, India could save the world, and secure its own freedom. This is propaganda for colonial loyalty, but it expresses itself in terms that have since become familiar in the postcolonial lexicon (the challenge of a war for national liberation, the reorientation of colonial centre and margin, the location of agency and resistance in the people, and so on).

Though it is a bizarre late twist in the story of Orwell's relations with the East – now he is urging Indians to remain loyal to the Empire, in order to secure their freedom – there is no doubt that he is sincere in what he says. He did believe (and he was right) that the defeat of the Fascist powers would be followed by the dismantling of the European empires in the East, however painful and protracted the process. Perhaps this can be seen as a more benign variation of the pattern found in his earlier writing about the relation between East and West; the moment of kinship and solidarity is to be followed by a resumption of distance that will allow each to occupy its own space, both of them freed from the deforming weight of an imperial bond or bondage with the other. He welcomed that process when towards the end of his life he saw it begin, with independence for India and Pakistan. He would have preferred a postcolonial world to be a postnationalist one. He had soon given up his hope that the British Empire could be transformed into a federation of socialist states (*CW* xii. 427), but he remained anxious that British rule would be replaced in postcolonial Asia, especially in the Indian subcontinent, by a reinstantiation of the kind of paranoid nationalism that had plunged the world into war in the previous decade. That, however, would be for people in the East to determine for themselves. Meanwhile it was his belief that the people who would benefit most unambiguously from the end of empire would be the British themselves, who would no longer be obliged to speak and think of themselves as different in kind and quality from others.

3

England

Eric Blair was 24 when he returned from Burma on home leave in August 1927. The following month he decided to resign from the Burma police. What was the country he had now returned to? In many ways, England was most vivid to him as the country of his fatherless childhood – 'I barely saw my father before I was eight,' he was to remember (*CW* xviii. 316) – rather than of his youth. Raymond Williams describes Orwell's upbringing as 'in important ways strange and even alien' by the standards of most people's lives.[1] From 1911 to 1921 he had been at private boarding schools, first at St Cyprian's in Eastbourne, briefly at Wellington, and then for four and a half years at Eton. These schools were a self-contained world, as well as an exclusive one, for the boys who attended them. Home was a place to spend the holidays. Then came the five years in the tropics, in the imperial police. At the age of 24 Orwell had come back to a home country he did not know very much about. And, although England was to become one of the most important topics of his writing, he would retain a certain awkwardness, an uncomfortable fit in 'England your England' (*CW* xii. 392–409). This sense of questionable belonging was familiar enough among people, usually a lot older than 24, who had retired home after service in the colonies. But his own early experience of expatriation also gives him something in common with the great cosmopolitan modernists, of the generation of Joyce and Eliot; and so does his restlessness, not only the tramping but the bewildering array of the addresses where he lived, never for very long. He was to try in various ways to understand, penetrate, and even to bury himself in England. But he knew what the place looked like from the outside; this makes him eccentric, outside the centre. In his imagination he was always able to see England from the East, and this meant that he never lost sight of what it was, an imperial nation. It is the former colonial official who, for example, reminds his readers that 'the overwhelming bulk of the British proletariat does not live in Britain, but in Asia and Africa' (*CW* xi. 360).

Because all this gave him a defamiliarizing point of view, usefully aslant to the national life, Orwell's evocations of England always have a tinge of research in them. This is true in an obvious way of *The Road to Wigan Pier* and the documentary detail of *Down and Out in Paris and London*, but it is also a feature of his journalistic essays on aspects of English life like seaside postcards (and sexual politics) in 'The Art of Donald McGill', pubs in 'The Moon under Water', the heroes and myths of 'Boys' Weeklies' and their ideological implications, 'A Nice Cup of Tea', and 'In Defence of English Cooking'. Many of these essays anticipate the sort of work on popular culture that is more ponderously done under the contemporary rubric of Cultural Studies. Often they display a capacity to be surprised by discoveries in the commonplace, which again testifies to Orwell's slightly dislocated point of view.

But the most ambitious of his studies in the anthropology of England were done in fiction, in the sequence of three novels about English life that he wrote in the 1930s. In each of these can be traced the developments and sometimes contradictions of Orwell's ideas through the decade, and each is linked in quite intimate ways to his own experience. But taken together (and especially with the crucial non-fictional interruption of *The Road to Wigan Pier*), they begin to take the shape of a project whose topic is contemporary England. They deal with social institutions and problems, through the medium of personal stories and the drama of character. *A Clergyman's Daughter* is concerned with the family, the Church, and school, and with people who are most neglected and exploited in a society without feeling. *Keep the Aspidistra Flying* is metropolitan, it satirizes the world of writing and publishing and the disaffection of the intellectual, and considers the relation between a snobbish high culture and the vulgar commercial world. And *Coming Up for Air* anatomizes the changing world of the provincial and suburban middle class, the fate of the pre-war England of Orwell's own childhood, and a gathering sense of panic under the shadow of another war. From the alarm clock that explodes 'like a horrid little bomb' at the beginning of *A Clergyman's Daughter*, to the actual bomb that falls on Lower Binfield at the end of *Coming Up for Air*, these novels sketch the beleaguered condition of England in the 1930s.

However inchoate his political ideas at this time, Orwell had brought back from colonial Burma a simple and serviceable idea of how society worked: one kind of people rather nervously held power over another kind. In the East the powerless greatly outnumbered the powerful, and there was a visible racial difference between them; and this difference was held to be the justification for the privilege of one kind over the other. When in *Down and Out in Paris and London* (1933) he applied this colonial model to Europe, Orwell could see, of course, that class was not the same thing as race, but he felt that class in the West operated *like* race in the East in the way that people thought about others. 'Fear of the mob is a superstitious fear. It is based on the idea that there is some mysterious, fundamental difference between rich and poor, as though they were different races, like negroes and white men' (*D&O* 121). Economic differences were naturalized in people's minds – they were felt to be essential, unquestionable, in the order of things – and although 'a tramp is only an Englishman out of work' (*D&O* 205), some Englishmen, in the eyes of society, were less English than others. Beggars are 'ordinary human beings' doing a job of work, he says, but in England they are orientalized, treated as 'a race apart' (*D&O* 174). The belief that the poor were essentially different was an unjust and dehumanizing superstition. Orwell was not yet quite ready to translate this discovery back into the language of racial difference.

The down and outs of Paris and London were unambiguously below the line dividing power and privilege from their opposites. The line is just as firmly drawn in the novel *A Clergyman's Daughter* (1935), but here it is mapped in a more nuanced way. Orwell's first fictional account of England focuses on a character who comes from and returns to the shabby-genteel impoverished professional lower upper-middle class, Orwell's own. And his first fictional embodiment of England is a woman.

The first part of *A Clergyman's Daughter* is schematic, almost allegorical, in its portrayal of English provincial life. Dorothy Hare keeps house for her widower father, the rector of Knype Hill in Suffolk, and does 'the dirty work of the parish' (*CD* 18), just as Orwell was to describe himself doing 'the dirty work of empire' in Burma.[2] The rector is a mean and snobbish patriarch who bullies his daughter and despises his parishioners. He is the younger son of the younger son of a baronet, lives in the splendour of an imaginary past, and makes stupid and dwindling investments in far-flung enterprises like Sumatra Tin and United Celanese, while Dorothy is obliged to run the household in debt to local tradesmen. Morning communion in the draughty church attracts a congregation of two, including Dorothy. Lord Pockthorne owns a fifth of the county, and Mr Blifil-Gordon owns the local sugar-beet refinery and is the Conservative candidate for election. Mr Warburton the local artist is a selfish dilettante who never does any work, and tries to seduce Dorothy. So much for family, religion, politics, and art. For history and culture, there is the awful school play, *Charles I*, and later a pageant of English history, for which Dorothy labours to make the costumes with glue and brown paper. (Orwell himself had written and directed a school play, *Charles II*, when he was teaching at The Hawthorns in Hayes, Middlesex, at Christmas 1932.) And Knype Hill performs its ceaseless and futile autobiography in the circulation of malicious gossip, usually at the expense of women.

Harvest Festival is in the offing when the story starts, but the keynote of Knype Hill is barrenness. There is no issue and there seems to be no escape. Dorothy is oppressed in the household and burdened with Christian guilt. She is afraid of sex, and is in the habit of sticking a pin into her flesh to expiate any unworthy thought, in complicity with her own subjection. It is a positive relief when she turns up in a London street, at the beginning of part two, having lost her memory and identity after some kind of breakdown (such is her subjection that she can make her escape only when the habits of consciousness are suspended). She falls in with a group of vagrants and, when they all go down to Kent to earn some money in the hop harvest, we have returned to the world of *Down and Out*. Though this is still a third-personal narrative, with privileged access to Dorothy's consciousness, it slips often into the kind of sociological-documentary mode of *Down and Out*, carefully noting details of the hop-pickers' pay, workload, conditions, food, and so on. Working in the hop fields, Dorothy does acquire a precarious life of her own, but there is little festive about this harvest of alienated labour, and when the season is over she is no further forward, though she has now recovered her memory. She drifts back to London, and is soon destitute and homeless, with winter approaching.

The third part gives an account of a single freezing night Dorothy spends in Trafalgar Square with some dozen other homeless people. Here the narrative suddenly disappears, to be replaced by dramatic dialogue, demotic and sometimes surreal. It is a striking and important moment in Orwell's writing, as the destitute grumble and shiver through the merciless night, finally piling together for warmth on a bench 'in a monstrous shapeless clot, men and women clinging indiscriminately together, like a bunch of toads at spawning time' (*CD* 174). These are the last people in London, and for a while Dorothy is an indistinguishable component of this human heap. They have no possessions at all except their voice, and to tell their story Orwell recognizes that he has to allow them to speak for themselves. So the controlling narrative voice falls silent, and a chattering polyphony takes over – the vagrants, streetwalkers, a defrocked parson, the old and the imbecile, huddled together in 'the horrible communism of the Square' (*CD* 185–6).

After the technically conservative opening movements of the novel, Orwell is suddenly lining himself up with avant-garde fiction here in the Trafalgar Square chapter. The model is clearly the Nighttown chapter of Joyce's *Ulysses*, though in interesting ways Orwell's London night also looks like a parodic underground reply to the London day of Virginia Woolf's *Mrs Dalloway*. The polyphony of the dispossessed recapitulates themes from the first half of the book, such as the loss of faith, sex and scandal, broken families, class prejudice, as well as destitution, hunger, and crime. Interestingly, though, Orwell cannot sustain the formal revolution that allows his huddled mass of characters to speak for themselves. As happens quite often in his early work (and the comparison with the routine boldness of *Ulysses* shows this up very clearly), he seems to lose his nerve. The 'stage directions' get longer, and turn into narrative, and by the end of the chapter the Orwell narrator is back in control with his omniscience, his normative literary English, and his heroine soon to be returned to a version of middle-class existence. The problem, of how the disadvantaged can be represented or represent themselves, remained, in its political and artistic dimensions.

Having made common cause, at first involuntarily and even unconsciously, with the dispossessed, and for a while joined their chorus, Dorothy comes to her senses and returns to her own class and its habitual language (and the novel that tells her story to its traditional bourgeois mode). That intimation of kinship, like the one in the prison yard in 'A Hanging', has a time limit, for she cannot long escape from who she really is. There is a similar pattern in the next chapter, when she gets work as a teacher in Mrs Creevy's ghastly school for girls. She tries to turn the school 'from a place of bondage into a place human and decent' (*CD* 214), and encourages the girls to think and speak and work for themselves. For a short while she succeeds in persuading at least some of them that she is on their side. This, however, is certainly not what either the parents or the proprietor have in mind, and Dorothy is soon bullied back into teaching the soulless curriculum of copybook handwriting and arithmetic (especially money sums). It has often been pointed out that Orwell's fiction, from *Burmese Days* to *Nineteen Eighty-Four*, tells and retells the story of a failed attempt to escape from various forms of oppression. By the end of *A Clergyman's Daughter* the circle closes on Dorothy Hare, back where she started in her father's house, her original place of bondage, and now even without religious faith to sustain her. Dorothy is Orwell's most hapless character because she is most helpless and most alone. In this England, everything bears down upon the woman. Orwell was to remark later that, though civilization rested on slavery for 5,000 years or more, we know the names of scarcely a handful of individuals among those countless generations of slaves (*CW* xvi. 305–6). With Dorothy Hare, facing in the end an unfulfilled life of unpaid drudgery and thankless exploitation, Orwell gives a name to a kind of slavery, which is slavery no less for the complicity of the woman who does not want to escape.

A Clergyman's Daughter is an ungainly book, however. The amnesia device is contrived and melodramatic, and the transitions are awkward. Part of the problem lies in the young Orwell's determination to extract fictional copy from his own experience, such as the hop picking and the schoolteaching. As late as 1948 he was to confess, in a letter: 'One difficulty I have never solved is that one has masses of experience which one passionately wants to write about . . . and no way of using them up except by disguising them as a novel' (*CW* xix. 336). Another weakness can be seen in the way the novel's two most interesting features – Dorothy's domestic bondage, and the heaped bodies and voices, like something from Dante's *Inferno*, in the Trafalgar Square chapter – point to the double motivation or agenda of the book, the exposure of social injustice and the individual bourgeois tragedy not yet convincingly integrated in Orwell's mind. His next novel, while again drawing on some of his own experience (his 'Bookshop Memories' (*CW* x. 510–13) and his struggles as an unknown writer in London), centres on a much more articulate character, who is all too ready to make connections between his individual plight and the social and economic conditions in which it is played out.

Dorothy Hare was not quite 28 when her story began. Gordon Comstock, hero or anti-hero of *Keep the Aspidistra Flying* (1936), is 29, but looks older. (And Orwell was 33 when his third novel was published.) The first thing we are told about Gordon is that he is the last of his line; with him the Comstock family seems doomed to sterile extinction. Haunted romantically by the fear that his creative powers are drying up, he is associated with images of sterility and morbidity, as he acknowledges with gloomy relish. His first book of poems, entitled *Mice*, is 'dead as a blasted foetus in a bottle' (*KAF* 92); London itself, he thinks fashionably, is like a city of the dead. Gordon courts failure, and sees no escape; his demoralized predicament, like the circularity of Dorothy Hare's travels, seems to signal an entropic failure to *get* anywhere, a lack of agency to make narrative. 'Year in, year out, *nothing ever happened* in the Comstock family' (*KAF* 66).

Still, Gordon is a livelier and much more articulate protagonist than Dorothy, though this may be because, as an only son, he has been educated at the expense of his widowed mother's health and his dismal sister's opportunities in life. It is an education that has left him opinionated, idealistic, egotistical, and for most practical purposes useless. The novel shows him to be selfish, ungrateful, pompous, and occasionally cruel, but he is the cleverest of Orwell's anti-heroes. *A Clergyman's Daughter* had been a strange choice of subject, since Orwell did not care much about the Church and knew rather little of women (he had spent most of his time in all-male communities from prep school to the Burma police), but in the world of Gordon Comstock he was on home ground, the modern Grub Street of the struggling young writer he himself was. Consequently the narrative can never quite decide on its point of view on this protagonist, whether it wants to identify with Comstock's views or to mock them. Comstock's work sounds very much like the poems that occasionally appeared in Middleton Murry's *Adelphi*, over the name of E. A. Blair.[3] His modernist disaffection – 'Look at all these bloody houses, and the meaningless people inside them!' (*KAF* 94) – his lack of faith, and his taste for sordid urban realism, mark him as an admirer of the early T. S. Eliot; his contempt for bourgeois vulgarity and philistinism is modernist too. Orwell knew all about these things, as he knew about the miserable conditions of Gordon's day-to-day existence: the squalid lodgings, the sex starvation, the demeaning arithmetic of scrimping and cadging, the prickly vanity of the unsuccessful author. In fact, Gordon's is a bohemian rather than an absolute poverty, since it is clear that he could always go back to the well-paid job he has renounced in the world of commercial advertising. Nonetheless, while it lasts, his resistance to materialism has a comic magnificence that is only partly spoiled by his relentless self-pity.

Gordon Comstock's London is in the grip of the drab austerities of the Depression, the stagnation of political life under a National Government that had in effect disenfranchised the entire electorate by depriving them of meaningful choice, the antagonisms and anxieties of class, the stirrings of nervousness about a coming war. No wonder he never finishes his grand poem *London Pleasures*; London hardly seems to afford any. Nonetheless, *Keep the Aspidistra Flying* is an important novel of London life. When Gordon Comstock walks the city streets – as he often does, because it is free, and it keeps you warm – it is the city of Orwell's own impoverished early struggles to make it as a writer. This novel is Orwell's only fictional portrait of the artist – though its Joycean affinities are really with *Dubliners* – and there is more than a titular connection between the city and the 'scrawled, grimy labyrinth of words' that is Comstock's unfinished opus, sole product of a thousand hours' work (*KAF* 244).

In this book England is the metropolis, with a brief would-be romantic excursion into the countryside – the same geography as in *Nineteen Eighty-Four*. But the city is a labyrinth of words as well as of streets. The novel (itself a city of words) thinks of England in terms of language. Its central character is of course a language man, a poet, a bookseller, a copywriter, a twopenny librarian. Words are his element. But the story of Gordon Comstock and his struggles is the dramatic foreground of a picture of England in which class, money, and culture perform an intricate dance; and the trope that Orwell lit upon to show how this worked was a conflict not between characters but between kinds of English, or, more accurately, between uses of literacy.

Keep the Aspidistra Flying is all about reading and writing. Gordon Comstock is a writer who earns a living selling other people's books. He has quit a job writing advertising copy for consumer goods like breakfast cereal and QT Sauce. He uses his idle time in the bookshop to compose a poem; through the shop window he can see an advertising poster, and the poster gets into the poem. His toffish friend Ravelston publishes Gordon's work in his magazine *Antichrist* and vainly urges him to read Marx, but later Gordon stops writing poetry and will read nothing but weekly papers, which Orwell lists lovingly – *Tit Bits, Answers, Peg's Paper, The Gem, The Magnet, Home Notes, The Girl's Own Paper.*

When his girlfriend Rosemary tells him she is pregnant, it is a visit to the lending library that helps him decide what he wants to do about it; he marries her, and goes back to composing commercial slogans.

The cultural plot of *Keep the Aspidistra Flying* can be examined in terms of a contest between discourses (I use the term here to indicate a large body of statements and language habits, emanating from a group or institution, and embodying a set of values that constitutes a view of the world). The two principal antagonists are the discourse of poetry and the imagination, and the discourse of commerce and consumption.

Gordon Comstock is a poet with a romantic dedication to his art, though his creative labours have hitherto produced only the stillborn *Mice*. The institutions of literature in the novel are not impressive. Gordon pathetically cherishes one favourable review in the *Times Literary Supplement*, Ravelston's magazine publishes the work of poets he feels sorry for, and in bookshop and library Gordon purveys middlebrow comfort reading and popular trash to a reading public he despises. (Q. D. Leavis's *Fiction and the Reading Public* (1932) sheds some light on this world and on some of Comstock's opinions.) Hardly anyone reads Comstock. 'Poetry! The last futility' (*KAF* 38). But he clings stubbornly to his vocation, for he sees poetry, in spite or because of its odour of failure and absurdity, as offering almost the last resistance to its mighty opposite, the language of money. The antagonism of these two discourses is built into every level of the novel. From Gordon's point of view, '*all* modern commerce is a swindle' and 'Money is what God used to be' (*KAF* 46); and he chooses the futility rather than the swindle, as Winston Smith will do after him. The politics of *Keep the Aspidistra Flying* is linguistic. There is an uneven struggle between these two discourses for the soul of England. It drives the plot – can the bohemian and moth-eaten poet hold out against bourgeois materialism? It is in the narrative too. One chapter begins with a careless heap of some of the usual invocations of spring from the English poetic tradition – 'Bytuene Mershe ant Averil, when spray beginneth to spring', 'the hounds of spring are on winter's traces', and so on – but 'if it was spring Gordon failed to notice it' (*KAF* 248), and soon he is back to prosaic work on an advertising campaign for

April Dew, a deodorant. The language of advertising is the novel's metonymy for the discourse of money, because advertising is the agent of conformity that persuades people to think of themselves primarily as consumers, especially if they are or aspire to be middle class, and enrols them, rich or poor, as disciples of the money god.

The institution that serves and circulates this discourse is the advertising agency called, not very subtly, the New Albion. On street hoardings it propagates its own kind of poetry – 'Roland Butta enjoys his meal with Bovex' (*KAF* 4) – which, unlike Gordon's, everybody reads, every day. (At the publisher's insistence, 'Roland Butta' was renamed and became 'Corner Table' in the original edition. The big-brotherly image of this consumer avatar is omnipresent in the novel. Gordon Comstock himself is far from the ideal consumer; his two worst disasters involve reckless eating and drinking.) Adverts, for products from Roughage for Husky Kids to the World-Famed Culturequick Scrapbook, provide a sort of cross section of the money world, thinks Gordon, 'a panorama of ignorance, greed, vulgarity, snobbishness, whoredom and disease' (*KAF* 262). This discourse sells not just consumer products but lifestyle and ultimately values, the values Gordon scornfully associates with the aspidistra, that bourgeois fetish. And a powerful discourse can dictate people's sense not only of what is valuable, but of what is real. If this is the 'real' England, Gordon is thoroughly estranged in it. The 'yard-wide faces' of the ad posters cancel him out, and drain his petulant rebellion and his weak poetry of reality. In serious ways *Keep the Aspidistra Flying* is a comic prefiguration of *Nineteen Eighty-Four*, and the discourse tyranny of Ingsoc is anticipated in the language of the aspidistra, commodity fetishism, and bourgeois conformity.

There is a third force to be reckoned with in the novel, and it is not the earnest Marxism of Ravelston (which derives from the familiar 1930s syndrome Christopher Isherwood called 'rentier guilt'), for neither Gordon nor apparently Orwell is willing to take it seriously. Socialism is for adolescents – 'At that age one does not see the hook sticking out of the rather stodgy bait' (*KAF* 46) – and a socialist society as Gordon envisages it would be an unacceptably boring alternative to the money world. The third force is associated with Rosemary, and we shall have to call it a paradiscourse, since it appears to be substantially non-linguistic.

Gordon and Rosemary often argue, but she is most persuasive when she is silent. 'She lay quiet, content to argue no longer, her arms round him like a sleepy siren. The woman-scent breathed out of her, a powerful wordless propaganda against all altruism and all justice' (*KAF* 109). This somewhat disturbing passage shows Rosemary embodying the enticing pragmatism of the flesh, and it is to this strong persuasion that Gordon eventually succumbs, after Rosemary becomes pregnant, settling down to respectability, marriage, and parenthood. This after all, it seems, is the 'real' world, the life of the body and its continuity, actual rather than verbal London pleasures. In the face of it his resistance melts and his intellectual and artistic struggles recede. In its tender if evasive ending, *Keep the Aspidistra Flying* is at its furthest point from *Nineteen Eighty-Four*, where sexuality and the life of the body are agents not of reconciliation but of resistance, at least for a while.

Between *Keep the Aspidistra Flying* and his third novel about England, *Coming Up for Air* (1939), Orwell undertook two crucial journeys, to the north of England and to Spain, which resulted in two pivotal books, *The Road to Wigan Pier* and *Homage to Catalonia*. These will be discussed later. But, while holding to the usefulness of treating the three novels about England as a group, I need to emphasize that the third novel is in important ways set somewhat apart from the other two. The intervening years, from early 1936 to early 1939, had led Orwell to see England in a different light. His later attitude to these three books was different too. He dismissed *A Clergyman's Daughter* and *Keep the Aspidistra Flying* as botched work (although in fact he disparaged all of the books he wrote, at one time or another), but he seems to have had a somewhat less low opinion of *Coming Up for Air*, which was the first of his books chosen for printing in a uniform edition in 1948. (Still, most writers will find it extraordinary that, when his publisher Secker & Warburg needed the novel for resetting, Orwell discovered that he did not have a copy. He says they were obliged to steal one from a public library (*CW* xix. 336).) The novel comes after the political watershed of his career, 'the

Spanish war and other events in 1936–7', as Orwell himself identified it in 'Why I Write' (*CW* xviii. 319). Of the many implications of this change of vision, one large and simple one is particularly important for the portrayal of England in *Coming Up for Air*. It is a change that has to do with history.

Burmese Days is in a sense an ahistorical novel. That is, it deals with a historical phenomenon, British colonialism in the East, but it is essentially a static world that it depicts, with the triumph of the institutions and personnel that have an interest in keeping things as they are. The same might be said of *A Clergyman's Daughter*, with the circle of defeat that returns Dorothy to the service of Church and father after her adventures, as if nothing had happened; and of the futile circulations and rueful compromise that bring Gordon Comstock back to the New Albion and down to a blind-alley flat with an aspidistra in the window. But *Coming Up for Air* imagines an England that is dynamic, historicized. This does not mean that it has acquired a sense of the past – the inescapability of the past was one of the problems of the earlier novels, after all. *Coming Up for Air* is historical because it has a sense of the future, and that the future might be different. This perhaps was the chief lesson of Spain for Orwell, and it was by no means a reassuring discovery.

In *Coming Up for Air*, when George Bowling finally sets out on a June morning for the place where he spent his boyhood, he feels as if, behind his car, there is a huge army streaming up the road in pursuit. Orwell enjoyed making lists, and this is one of his liveliest. Bowling can see in his mind's eye this horde of spoilsports, led by his wife and family, his employers, neighbours with 'prams and mowing-machines and concrete garden-rollers', all trying to stop him getting away, and 'all the soul-savers and Nosey Parkers, the people who you've never seen but who rule your destiny all the same, the Home Secretary, Scotland Yard, the Temperance League, the Bank of England, Lord Beaverbrook, Hitler and Stalin on a tandem bicycle, the bench of Bishops, Mussolini, the Pope – they were all of them after me' (*CUA* 182–3). History is a nightmare from which Bowling is trying to escape by returning to find the idyll of his childhood, hoping to find it unchanged. It is no surprise that, when he gets to Lower Binfield, history has got there before him. The 'deep, deep sleep of England', invoked at the end of *Homage to Catalonia*, has been violently broken.

The new vision of England required a new kind of protagonist. Hitherto Orwell had placed the centre of consciousness of his fictions on the margins of the community. Dorothy Hare and Gordon Comstock peered out from the corners of English society, from the vantage of the downtrodden and the bloody-minded, the bullied conformist and the peevish rebel. But George Bowling is a stakeholder. He is a middle-class, middle-aged, middlebrow middle Englander, the only one of Orwell's protagonists to be upwardly mobile, and the only one – at least his only human character – to retain a feeling for the community he has come from. 'It mightn't be a bad thing, if you could manage it, to feel yourself one of them, one of the ruck of men,' thinks Gordon Comstock, as he slinks back to the bourgeoisie (*KAF* 267). It is George Bowling's world he capitulates to, the world of clerks and shopkeepers and commercial travellers and motor salesmen. In turning for a subject to this world, which he had never taken seriously before, Orwell was also paying homage to its earlier chronicler and one of his own early literary heroes, the H. G. Wells of *Kipps* and *The History of Mr Polly*.

George Bowling stands foursquare for a certain traditional kind of Englishness, as his name – and perhaps even his initials – seem to suggest, but it is an Englishness that appears on the face of it to have adapted quite well to the modern world. Orwell provides the novel with a densely realized social context, perhaps in compensation for failing to furnish it with much of a plot. George's father was a retail seedsman in a small market town in the Thames Valley, and he himself has moved up in a modest way to be an insurance salesman with a house and a mortgage in the inner-outer suburbs. This shift from agrarian to suburban life is as socially momentous as any country boy's journey to the metropolis in a nineteenth-century novel; it indicates a form of modernity, an economic and a cultural change. George Bowling seems to be quite comfortable in this modern milieu, indeed he appears to be typical of it. He is good-humoured and gregarious, and narrates his story in an informal and friendly style that brings the reader into his world, assuming goodwill and inviting recognition. This style, though it is indifferent to matters of 'high culture', is otherwise close to the informal, sometimes apparently rambling discourse of Orwell's later journalism, especially in his 'As I Please' column for *Tribune*, with its habits of drawing the reader in to share his observations. If Bowling is typical, he also thinks in terms of types – 'one of those little stucco boxes' (*CUA* 11) is an example of his favourite construction – and he speaks to a reader who is a man like himself. 'Why did I marry her? you say. But why did you marry yours?' (*CUA* 140). He is thoroughly integrated into a stable world he thinks he knows well. The novel then seems to ask: if George Bowling is recognizable as middle England, what are his chances?

For there are increasingly alarming signs that George Bowling's world is not as stable as it looks. In fact it is coming to bits. It is not simply that, like almost everyone else in England in 1938, he knows there is another great war coming. You can compare George's household to his father's to see how traditional family ties have been weakened in the course of a generation. This is an ill-conditioned England, and nothing can be relied on. What looks like a frankfurter is actually made of fish. Even murder is not what it was.[4] A killing and dismemberment are reduced to the headline LEGS: FRESH DISCOVERIES, a prefiguration of the bomb blast in Lower Binfield at the end of the story – 'in among the broken crockery there was lying a leg. Just a leg, with the trouser still on it . . .' (*CUA* 235). In middle England, the centre is disintegrating. George Bowling's family itself, ironically enough, is a symptom of that disintegration, with the unhappy marriage of the failed seedsman's son to the daughter of a retired colonial official from 'the officer-rentier-clergyman class', accustomed to govern an empire, but now washed out (*CUA* 139).

Dorothy Hare and Gordon Comstock were younger than Orwell when he wrote about them; George Bowling is older. He belongs to the generation that came of age in 1914, and consequently he thinks of the First World War as the crucial event that has changed English life, destroying the reassuring natural rhythms of pre-war life, setting in motion a process of violent change that uproots communities and tears apart the landscape, and opens England up to a dehumanized future that will belong to 'the streamlined men who think in slogans and talk in bullets' (*CUA* 168–9). This dismemberment of English life George tries to counter by an act of remembering, in the form of a journey home. It is an attempt to take hold of a lost cultural identity, to remember who he is. In the shadow of a historical crisis, he is in effect mounting a single-handed nativist project, an effort to recover and reassert a traditional English way of life and its traditional values. He does not put it so pompously himself. His journey to Lower Binfield, which he comically has to keep as secret as an adulterous adventure, is a holiday, which he wants to spend on the favourite activity of his childhood, fishing. But, though a private and indeed secret resolution, it is a political gesture too, a 'coming up for air' before the plunge into the war that is certainly coming. The world of his childhood is remembered as peaceful and natural, and the future promises to be neither. 'Fishing', he explains to himself, 'is the opposite of war' (*CUA* 85).

But that is not strictly true. His most vivid memories of fishing are tied up with his desire to belong like his brother to the Black Hand gang, juvenile toughs whose pastimes include torturing animals and making fun of the village halfwit. What is more, the idyllic pre-war world of Lower Binfield – if it was idyllic, if it really existed – was already crumbling in the years of George Bowling's childhood. The boys go fishing in the neglected grounds of the great Queen Anne house at Binfield, which stands empty because the squire can no longer afford to live in it. And, as early as 1909, George's father's business, with those of other small local merchants, has begun to be overwhelmed by competition from the big-business suppliers Sarazins, 'universal poultry and livestock providers', with their huge advertisements and branches all over the Home Counties. Already before the First World War the forces of modernity were at work, transforming lives and landscape. These forces have simply gathered pace in George's lifetime, so that when he returns home he will find the numinous childhood places literally no longer there, and his own connections with the past, as one of 'the Bowlings of Lower Binfield', erased. The George, the pub where he stays and that shares his name, is unrecognizable, and so is he; nobody remembers him. If George can find no one to share his memory of the past, then it is as good or bad as a fantasy, and the values he associates with it, values of continuity and community and contentment, are sunk, to be replaced by a modern 'sense of disbelieving in everything' (*CUA* 128) – for all three of Orwell's novels about England centre on a loss of faith. In Binfield now, the only alternative to the vulgarity and greed of 'development' is the equally vulgar sentimentalism of a colony of faddists, 'the awful gang of food-cranks and spook-hunters and simple-lifers with £1000 a year', who refer to the Binfield beech woods as the Pixy Glen (*CUA* 228–9). Orwell's vehement hostility to 'cranks' is surprising, and was indiscriminate; in *The Road to Wigan Pier* he had grumbled that 'the mere words "Socialism" and "Communism" draw towards them with magnetic force every fruit-juice drinker, nudist, sandal-wearer, sex-maniac, Quaker, "Nature Cure" quack, pacifist and feminist in England' (*RWP* 161). If there is any value in George Bowling's England, it is not going to be found among faddists and cranks, nor in the blithe antiquarianism of his friend Porteous, nor in the bellicose rhetoric of left or right as the coming crisis darkens the horizon.

Coming Up for Air gives a conservative vision of English modernity, or would do if it had a stronger sense of what might be worth conserving, other than the doomed joys of childhood. The prognosis is gloomy indeed. Bowling can foresee a future of food queues, rubber truncheons, slogans, enormous faces. 'The bad times are coming, and the streamlined men are coming too. What's coming afterwards I don't know, it hardly even interests me' (*CUA* 239). Strangely enough, it is to the articulation of this voice, George Bowling's voice (even as it grumbles and digresses and blusters), that we have to look to find any sense of resistance to the gathering forces of that foreseen future. Bowling is far from heroic, and he is not particularly eloquent or outstandingly honest. But he is not taken in. He stands for something like the lowest common denominator of those values that Orwell was later, when the next war really came, to try to find in an embattled England, which made it still worth fighting for. Those values – 'decency' is the name Orwell most often finds for them – were to be discovered not in the lost history of Lower Binfield but in the inflections of an English voice. Less self-conscious, less tormented, and tougher than Orwell's earlier protagonists,

Bowling is the portly embodiment of England's conscience. It is significant that he is also his creator's only entirely fictional first-personal subject.

Towards the end of *Coming Up for Air*, there is a description of the accidental dropping of a bomb on Lower Binfield. One house has had its outer wall neatly ripped off, exposing to view an incongruously tidy bedroom, and a smashed scullery (the one with the severed leg). The exposure of interiority, both domestic and psychological, had been the main business of the English novel for a century and more, and with the end of *Coming Up for Air* Orwell puts it behind him. There were to be no more fictions of private life. Indeed he was to go on to imagine a near-future modernity in which in the end there would be no private life to write about or inhabit. But, although *Coming Up for Air* was his last novel about England, he had already published a non-fictional account of the 'condition of England' in *The Road to Wigan Pier* (1937). And part one of that book began and ended with the description of an English interior.

The interior of the Brookers' tripe shop and lodging house, where *The Road to Wigan Pier* comes to consciousness (it is early morning), is one of Orwell's most vigorous set pieces, evoked in all its discomfort and squalor with the same relentlessness as the dreary domestic amenities of Dorothy Hare or Gordon Comstock, or the kitchens and doss houses of *Down and Out*. The household is not only dirty, but mean. Its most revolting features are the signs not of poverty but of the landlord's greed and contempt for others. The Brookers are slatternly and lazy. They exploit their wretched lodgers, and cheat the welfare authorities. Their language seems to be as degraded as their domestic hygiene; their habit of saying the same things over and over again 'gives you the feeling that they are not real people at all' (*RWP* 14). In its way it is a memorable portrait, but it is not one that you would choose to illustrate a theme of the dignity of working people, nor (since the narrator, a middle-class visitor from the south of England, is the principal victim of the Brookers) their exploitation. It raises the question of what the narrator is doing, and what he is doing there. These are questions that open into the perennial Orwell issues of subjectivity and genre.

What Orwell was doing there, in fact, was fulfilling a commission from Victor Gollancz, who had published all his four books to date, to visit areas of mass unemployment in Lancashire and Yorkshire. He spent time in Wigan, Bradford, and Sheffield, gathering material. When the manuscript was submitted, Gollancz helped to get it selected as a Left Book Club (LBC) choice (he was one of the founders of the club, which was formed in February 1936 while Orwell was in Wigan). This ensured it a much wider sale than Orwell's previous work. Gollancz had sent Orwell north to report on the conditions of working people, and then chose the resulting book for distribution to members of a socialist reading club. It is clear that Orwell's fourth chapter, for instance, with its meticulous descriptions of working people's housing conditions, supported by tables and footnotes and statistics, would meet Gollancz's expectation. But it is less clear how the description of the Brookers' household forwards the cause of socialism or promotes solidarity between sympathetic southern readers and the northern poor, while much of the second part of the book filled Gollancz with such misgivings that he wrote a preface for the LBC edition, in which among other things he distances himself, and defends by implication the good readers of the Left Book Club, from Orwell's criticism of socialism in England.[5]

As for what he was doing, Orwell as usual was writing more than one kind of book. While he was happy to provide fuel for the discussion and dissemination of socialist ideas, Orwell was also a man of letters, and still thought of himself primarily as a novelist. The scene setting *chez* Brooker is novelistic. Meanwhile (and this was what worried Gollancz) his socialism was provisional and unfinished, and he was also using the book as an essay that tests his own 'approach to socialism', and his personal struggle with 'the terribly difficult issue of class' (*RWP* 113). A small example of the generic instability that results, and a famous moment in the book, comes in the first chapter, when he describes seeing from the train window a young woman on her knees on the freezing ground, trying to unblock a waste pipe. 'She knew well enough', he concludes, 'what was happening to her – understood as well as I did how dreadful a destiny it was to be kneeling there in the bitter cold, on the slimy stones of a slum backyard, poking a stick up a foul drain-pipe' (*RWP* 15). It is a moving moment, and no less so if one observes that Orwell had learned these prose cadences from the fine writing of the likes of Lytton Strachey, hardly a model of socialist realism. Further, the account he wrote at the time in his diary says that Orwell was in the alley way when he saw the woman, not in a train leaving town (*CW* x. 427). Whether you take this displacement as a literary or a propaganda refinement, there is, typically, an uncertainty about point of view; not about the image, but about the observer's modality, where he stands in relation to what he sees.

Orwell had seen poverty and hardship before. He gives a blistering description of the squalor endured in the supposedly temporary caravan colonies in many northern towns, noting that he has seen such conditions in the Far East; but these are English people, in an English climate (*RWP* 56–7), so that the same squalor means something different. Two other English interiors can illustrate the complicated relations between observer and scene, the literary writer and the political work. What most readers remember best about *The Road to Wigan Pier* is Orwell's account of going down a coal mine, in the second chapter. Here the characteristic out-of-place awkwardness is entirely to the point, as he stumbles, bent double and weeping with pain, along miles of underground passages leading to the coalface. The observer in the scene is the gangling intellectual who would not last more than a few weeks at this punishing and dangerous work, on which his life and culture depend. 'It is so with all kinds of manual work; it keeps us alive, and we are oblivious to its existence' (*RWP* 30). The coalfield is the English interior that does not get into novels, the actual interior of England. In the first chapter, the narrator had declared patronizingly that it was 'a kind of duty to see and smell such places' as the Brookers' household now and again (*RWP* 14). The second chapter begins to show what that duty of observation might entail.

The third interior is evoked at the end of the first part of the book, and clearly is there to balance the lodging house at the beginning. Here Orwell praises the 'sane and comely shape' of working-class family life in a time of steady work and good wages. He paints a generic picture of domestic life in the evening for the worker and his family, like a sketch for a modern-day version of Burns's poem 'The Cotter's Saturday Night'. A manual worker has a better chance of being happy than an 'educated' man, he says, and the working-class interior at its best is 'a good place to be in, provided that you can be not only in it but sufficiently *of* it to be taken for granted' (*RWP* 108). The anxiety about the status of 'you' in the scene is again characteristic. This is not some Wellsian socialist utopia, nor is it placed in the brutish realities of a distant pre-industrial past. Orwell says he is evoking the memory of working-class interiors as he sometimes saw them in his childhood before the war (*RWP* 109). So the scene of this working-class idyll is not in the industrial north at all, but presumably in the Thames valley, and it dates from a time before the mass unemployment and Depression that sent him to Wigan, and indeed before the outbreak of war in 1914 when Orwell was 11. What is the scene doing here? It is surely a memory of the only time in Orwell's life when he was not aware of class distinctions – this awareness began, he says, when he was not much more than 6 (*RWP* 117) – so that this vision of working-class paradise was made possible for him because at the time he himself did not know there *was* a working class, or that he was not part of it. If the worker's family home looks like a paradise, even if only in imagination, it is the observer's own childish innocence that gives him entry to it, before the fall into class consciousness (and its divisive and fallen language) exiles him from such scenes for ever. As such it is a crucial moment for Orwell – whether or not it records an actual experience of his childhood – and points forward to *Coming Up for Air*, and to moments in both *Animal Farm* and *Nineteen Eighty-Four*. More immediately it points to the second part of *The Road to Wigan Pier*, which traces Orwell's own history in that fallen world, and tries to imagine redemption from it.

'The road from Mandalay to Wigan is a long one and the reasons for taking it are not immediately clear' (*RWP* 113). The clumsiness of that sentence is again symptomatic. It is here in the second part of *The Road to Wigan Pier* that Orwell struggles to integrate the two major experiences of his life, his service in the East and his perception of the inequalities of England. It is probably Orwell's most subtle passage of narrative, but the autobiographical account that follows may be briefly summarized like this: he describes how he grew up, as a sufficiently typical member of the lower upper-middle class, to speak and think of himself as essentially different from and better than the Lower Orders (the 'natural' sign of their difference, he was taught, was their smell), who were consequently regarded as 'a race of enemies' (*RWP* 117); how, endowed with this touchy sense of superiority, he entered empire service like many of his class because in a colonial society 'it was so easy to play at being a gentleman' (*RWP* 115), but in time, turning against the despotism he served, he came home under the burden of an immense weight of guilt; how his thoughts then turned to the English working class, 'because they supplied an analogy' (*RWP* 138), as victims of injustice like the Burmese; and how, to expiate his guilt, he felt a desire to become somebody else – give everything away, change his name, start from nothing – a naive wish that led to his forays on the road as a tramp.

But to abolish class distinctions would mean abolishing a part of yourself. Class is not just a matter of money and work, he soon realizes, but also a matter of culture and language, a perception of oneself and others. To lose class consciousness, says Orwell, somebody like him would have to stop thinking of himself as middle class, while his entire cultural experience tells him that is who he is; likewise, to lose a sense of racial superiority, it would be necessary for a European to stop thinking of himself or herself as essentially different from an oriental, in spite of everything that conspired to speak of that difference, and to call it a natural one. Class was not the same thing as race, but injustice in Mandalay was the same thing as injustice in Wigan, and it was perceptions of class and racial difference that kept injustice in place. Class and racial difference were deeply inscribed in the language itself, which is why Orwell has so much to say in this book about what may seem the relatively trivial matter of class accents. It is difficult to get beyond class prejudice when you identify yourself with your class every time you open your mouth. Every variety of English is a language of class. It is not possible at a stroke – it may not be possible at all – to 'get outside the class-racket'

(*RWP* 150), but at least socialists see a point in trying, for there can never be justice for everybody while some human beings are considered to be more human than others. So one way to start would be to find a language in which socialism could speak to people, 'to find the word that would move them' (*RWP* 202). Orwell was to claim in 'Why I Write' that the rest of his career was devoted to this end. But much of it would be given over to exposing kinds of language that kept people oppressed, the manacles by which they forged their own oppression and that of others. The second part of *The Road to Wigan Pier* shows how England's 'class-racket' and 'coolie empire' were inextricably linked in Orwell's own ideological history, and thereafter he saw them as indivisible. You could neither find nor sincerely seek justice in Wigan without justice in Mandalay.

When *The Road to Wigan Pier* was published, Orwell was already in Spain. The next ten years and more of his thinking about England would be dominated by the threat of fascism and Hitler's war. The threat, naturally enough, brought into focus for Orwell some of the things he valued most in English life, and he began to describe himself as a patriot – in this he was reverting, as he recognized, to the traditional loyalty of his class – although not a nationalist; after Spain, he was both internationalist and anti-nationalist. In wartime and later, some of his best writing is in a series of articles in which he seems to be assembling a compendium of aspects of popular culture in which value of a particularly English kind might be found. These include his long essay of 1940 on the liberalism of Dickens (Dickens could still be thought of as belonging to popular culture by Orwell's generation), his account of the carnivalesque humour of seaside postcards in 'The Art of Donald McGill', published in *Horizon* in 1941, and a series of pieces, mostly in his 'As I Please' column in *Tribune*, on such things as English cooking, junk shops, popular songs, pubs, and urban gardening. What is evoked here is George Bowling's England rather than (for example) T. S. Eliot's, or Winston Churchill's. It is an England of popular behaviour, rather than of political institutions or of high-cultural productions. To be sure, it was an England disabled by an anachronistic class system, but it had a promising future, he wrote in 1944 in the unmemorable *The English People*, if only 'the ordinary English in the street can somehow get their hands on power' (*CW* xvi. 227).[6] If England was indeed 'a family with the wrong members in control', as he had defined it in 1941 (*CW* xii. 401), there was a clear and realistic remedy.

'Bourgeois' morality – mostly practised, he pointed out, by the working class – muddled through with a kind of pragmatic and Bowlingesque decency that was some sort of bulwark against the temptations of fascism (*CW* xvi. 200). But the English were very far from immune from fascism. Orwell repeatedly warned the left against an unwillingness to admit that socialism itself had totalitarian possibilities. As for English institutions, in 'Such, Such Were the Joys' he was to remember his prep school as a fascistic society in miniature, the pattern of school life being 'a continuous triumph of the strong over the weak' (*CW* xix. 378). At least at first, however, the outbreak of the war had seemed to present both a danger and an opportunity, and in 'My Country Right or Left' in 1940 he urges a commitment to the defeat of Hitler, hoping that later those same patriotic instincts can be harnessed to the service of an English revolution and a socialist state. In any case, in the social mobilization of total war, class barriers seemed to be coming down. A post-war England, to be worth fighting for, would have to be socialist, and necessarily it would have to be postcolonial too. But, as the war went on, Orwell watched the signs of class tribalism (advertisements for personal servants, evening dress, railings round private gardens in London squares) starting to creep back into the everyday life of the capital, a pattern that he had seen before, in Barcelona in 1937. And when a Labour government was returned in 1945, its commitment to granting independence to India was far from assured: when the Labour Party Conference in 1945 approved a motion calling for independence for India, it did so against the advice of the party's executive. Orwell did not mind making the point again: 'Britain cannot become a genuinely Socialist country while continuing to plunder Asia and Africa' (*CW* xvii. 340). Britain was the name of the state and proprietor of the Empire. Orwell almost always refers to England when speaking of the nation and the culture. English can describe an ethnicity, British a citizenship.

Most of Orwell's political predictions during the war were wrong, as he acknowledged (*CW* xvi. 412). But he did understand that Hitler's war spelled the end, if not the immediate end, of the British Empire. Fascism and empire were not the same thing, but both were based on a view of the world that divided human beings into categories and assumed the right of one group to oppress the other on the grounds of innate superiority. In other words, both systems were racist and (using the term in Orwell's sense) nationalist; both were symptoms of what he called 'the race hatred and mass delusions which are part of the pattern of our time' (*CW* xix. 24). It is interesting that he often turns in his later journalism to questions of racism. He looked forward to an England devoted to social justice, and without an empire. He did not foresee that one result of the dismantling of empire would be the demographic mix of postcolonial (and theoretically multicultural) England. But he did understand that the point of ending empire was to free both the former colonialists and the former colonized from the nasty fantasies of racism, so as to make justice a possibility.

4

Europe

To the young Orwell, the world beyond England consisted of the colonies and Europe (there is no mention of the USA in his surviving writings before the summer of 1939). The England of his privileged if insecure upbringing was a place of the most complex and almost ineffable strata of prestige, but more crudely perceived as unequally divided in class terms, between Them and Us. The empire beyond the seas was a yet cruder reduplication of the hierarchies of the home country. Although Orwell could not resist pointing out that most of the European men he encountered in Burma would not have been classed as 'gentlemen' at home (*RWP* 132), the colonial East was a society of two kinds of people, white men and natives, with a great gulf fixed between them. We can begin to understand what continental Europe meant to Orwell if we see it first in negative terms, as he did, a place neither English nor colonial, where a different form of life might be possible. He left the Indian Imperial Police on 1 January 1928, and in the spring of that year he went to live in Paris. He was 24.

He had already made the first of his expeditions into the East End of London, and in *The Road to Wigan Pier* he was to explain how at this time of his life he felt compelled to expiate his load of guilt at his part in 'the dirty work of empire', by plunging into the underworld of poverty, getting down among the oppressed, and making common cause with them. But this does not seem to be a completely plausible motivation for his Paris adventure, if we judge by the account he gives in *Down and Out in Paris and London*, his first book, published by Gollancz in 1933. It is more likely that his disaffection with the work of empire became politically articulate during his time in

France, not before, and that the more immediate reason for his migration was vocational: the life of the artist could be more convincingly led in Paris than in Suffolk or Notting Hill. His tailor's records show that he went to Paris well-dressed,[1] and he seems to have been more of a dandy than a down and out, as long as his savings lasted. About half of the Parisian section of the book deals with the narrator's work as a scullion in the Hôtel X, and on the basis of this it offers some serious if diffident analysis of the psychology and politics of poverty and wealth. Most of the rest of the Paris section evokes life in the rue du Coq d'Or, 'a ravine of tall leprous houses' (*D&O* 1) in a working-class district, where the narrator lodges, cheek by jowl with a floating population of other impoverished and often eccentric 'characters', mostly foreigners like himself.

Here we have a catalogue of sketches and anecdotes, many self-contained and often in the words of the characters themselves. These people are poor, and after he has been robbed the narrator too experiences poverty. But, unlike Orwell's later reports on working-class life in the depressed north of England, his account of the life of the Parisian street dwells on the colourful, the raffish, the comic, and melodramatic. Most of the inhabitants of the rue du Coq d'Or are not French, and the ones we see most of, like Charlie with his lurid story of the rape of a prostitute, and the Russian Boris whose parents were killed in the Revolution – and indeed the narrator himself – are members of a more affluent class, fallen on hard times. This is *la vie de Bohème*, halfway between the Paris of *Trilby* and that of Henry Miller's *Tropic of Cancer* (1934). What is the Orwell narrator doing there? We know less about him than about even quite minor characters in the street. There is an odd diffidence about both his artistic and his political motivation; in fact there is something like a denial of both, so that in the end it is not at all clear why he is there. We learn that he gives English lessons; he lets slip to Boris that he 'goes in for writing' (*D&O* 22). Besides occasional journalism, in Paris Orwell wrote several stories and at least one novel, now lost. But *Down and Out* has nothing to say about writing. He does extract copy from his surroundings and neighbours – naively explaining that he has described Charlie, for example, 'just to show what diverse characters could be found flourishing in the Coq d'Or quarter' (*D&O* 11) – but he feels the necessity to explain at the end of the first chapter that Poverty itself is his theme; but claims to have no political opinions; yet has been in trouble with the police after being spotted coming out of the office of a Communist weekly paper.

There is a strangely touching and almost adolescent shyness about the narration of the early parts of the book, which no doubt reflects accurately enough the confusions of Orwell's own unformed political and aesthetic identity, and his indecision about the kind of book he thought he was writing. His Paris is partly a glamorously hand-to-mouth cosmopolitan bohemia, with its chess games and cheap wine and dodging the rent, and partly a grim underworld of migrant workers, hunger, unemployment, and explosions of violence. As the book progresses, the gaiety diminishes and the colours become sombre. Among the poor in the rue du Coq d'Or he seemed at first to have found a noisy daily egalitarianism that was a long way from his life in both England and Burma, and an easy comradeship that in some ways anticipates his experience of Barcelona in 1936. But these were 'the suburbs, as it were, of poverty' (*D&O* 15), and it was after all a life he had freely chosen. Once necessity closes in and he begins his career as a *plongeur*, washing the dishes in a hotel kitchen, his Paris can no longer be construed as a place of liberation in any sense. It takes on the contours of oppression in particularly familiar ways. No longer bohemian, it becomes oriental.

Bohemian Paris may be the garret and the café, but there is always access to the street and its teeming life. But the Paris of oppression has an enclosed and subterranean geography, the revolting kitchens beneath the luxury hotel where the narrator goes to work, and the 'secret vein of dirt, running through the great garish hotel like the intestines through a man's body' (*D&O* 80). The Hôtel X is almost embarrassingly symbolic of social inequality, with its grandiose classical façade and luxury fittings, and the miles of dark, labyrinthine corridors below, like 'the lower decks of a liner' (a memory of the passage to Burma, which remained one of Orwell's paradigms of an unjust society) (*D&O* 54). The kitchen is an infernal region, low ceilinged and stifling. Sometimes he has to work washing up in a filthy little scullery adjoining the dining room. 'There sat the customers in all their splendour – spotless table-cloths, bowls of flowers, mirrors and gilt cornices and painted cherubim; and here, just a few feet away, we in our disgusting filth' (*D&O* 67). As in the East, the servants are close, yet invisible, to the masters.

You can watch Orwell applying his knowledge of a familiar system to his understanding of a new one, an application that may have been made almost irresistible by the fact that the customers of the hotel were mostly Americans and English, foreign to the place and in most cases ignorant of the language. If memories of colonial Burma illuminate the life of the hotel, it is possible that the hotel also clarified his understanding of Burma, for here he was able to see and experience the system from beneath, in a way that had not been possible for even the most sympathetic European in the East. There are different occupations for different nationalities, and he describes an elaborate caste system among the hotel staff, whose prestige is graded as accurately as that of soldiers, with the scullions at the bottom, below even the chambermaids. The *plongeur*'s work is exhausting, demeaning, and miserably rewarded, part of a system that overcharges customers for a shoddy imitation of luxury they do not really want in the first place. What if the exploited should turn against the exploiters? It was a question that was to haunt *Burmese Days*. Orwell's answer here is a startling one. The downtrodden will not rebel because they cannot think. 'If *plongeurs* thought at all, they would long ago have formed a union and gone on strike for better treatment. But they do not think, because they have no leisure for it; their life has made slaves of them' (*D&O* 117). They were just like rickshaw-pullers or gharry-ponies in the East, he thought, ground down by bodily labour so that they had no mental energy, and lived a kind of animal existence. Their physical activity drained off their political agency, depriving them of the capacity to change their lives. Unremitting labour was a discipline that kept them docile. Their work could easily have been made more efficient, but if they had more leisure they would be more dangerous in the eyes of their employers. Released from their underground labours, they might soon transform themselves into the mob, which had played such an alarming part in the history of the city (and had been an anxiety, too, to the colonial policeman).

In these ways, Orwell orientalizes what he describes as 'the social significance of the *plongeur*'s life' (*D&O* 117) in order to understand it in terms of a paradigm he was familiar with from the other side, the side of authority and order and oppression. The relationship he described was not even a rational exploitation of one group by another, but stemmed from an emotional panic, a superstition like racism. The rich kept the poor at a distance, and kept them under, busy at useless work, because they feared them, believing them to be fundamentally and naturally different and therefore dangerous. This difference was a fantasy – for 'the average millionaire is only the average dishwasher dressed in a new suit' (*D&O* 121) – but, so long as the distance was maintained, so would the fantasy be. And at this point, having delivered the most sustained passage of political thinking of his career so far, Orwell loses his nerve, betraying the other side of his narrator's social gaucherie – for not only is he unsure of how he stands in relation to the Parisian poor whose life he shares, but he is also still uncertain of his standing with that other community, his English readers. Perhaps he has gone too far, or not far enough? 'These are only my own ideas about the basic facts of a *plongeur*'s life, made without reference to immediate economic questions, and no doubt largely platitudes. I present them as a sample of the thoughts that are put into one's head by working in a hotel' (*D&O* 122).

Traces of that shyness, that unformed literary identity, can be found on the front cover of Orwell's first book. 'Days in London and Paris' had been abandoned as a title, and in due course so was 'A Scullion's Diary', and 'Lady Poverty', and 'Confessions of a Dishwasher'. *Down and Out in Paris and London* followed a suggestion by the publisher Gollancz, though the author was uncomfortable with it. Page proofs survive with the authorial pseudonym 'X', but eventually the book was published under the name of 'George Orwell'. It seems to have been a last-minute decision, but it was also in some sense a premature one; George Orwell was not yet quite sure who he was.

His next visit to Paris was at the end of 1936, *en route* to Spain. By this time George Orwell was the author of five books, including the just-finished *The Road to Wigan Pier*, which told the story of his 'approach to socialism'. That book had reported on an England painfully divided, south from north and rich from poor, an economic division entrenched by culture and education and encoded in every syllable of English speech. He had gone on to read his own cultural history and identity, and their implication in these divisions, in an attempt to free his own mind and bring himself to the threshold of political action. But he was most vividly to see that action not in England but in Spain.

When in 1936 units of the army under Franco mounted a *coup d'état* against the left-wing republican government of Spain, the ensuing civil war was widely seen as a conflict between democracy and fascism. Orwell was one of many left-wing sympathizers across Europe who hurried to offer support, and in some cases to fight, for the republican cause (other individuals from outside Spain, in smaller numbers, supported the rebels). Fascist Germany and Italy aided and armed Franco, while the Soviet Union backed the Republic. Other European governments would not intervene. British literary leftists, among whom Orwell counted himself, felt that the struggle in Spain was theirs too. In this internationalism they were encouraged by the call for a Popular Front, formulated at the 1935 Congress of the Communist Third International or Comintern, which had urged all progressive political forces in Europe to unite against the common enemy of fascism. Orwell went to Spain, he said, with some notion of writing newspaper articles, but joined the militia almost immediately, 'because at the time and in that atmosphere it seemed the only conceivable thing to do' (*HC* 2).

'On that arid square,' W. H. Auden wrote in his poem 'Spain 1937', 'Our fever's menacing shapes are precise and alive.' Spain seemed to epitomize dramatically what was wrong with Europe, and particularly the conflict and division between right and left, between the privileged and the exploited, which Orwell had been writing about in *The Road to Wigan Pier*. But it was not conflict and division that Orwell encountered when he arrived in Barcelona. It was community, and it seemed to be a community of equals. He had never seen anything like it and it changed his life. He had come to report on the Spanish Civil War and he stayed to play a part in the Catalonian revolution.

Later he would admit that the revolution was not as complete or as admirable as it had seemed. Privilege and profit had not been eradicated in Barcelona in 1936, but were lying low; before long he was to see them reappear in the streets. And the two main revolutionary tendencies, the anarcho-syndicalists and the communists, were in uneasy alliance and would soon be at each other's throats. But for a while in those few weeks at the turn of 1936–7, it seemed that a good society, based on principles of equality and justice and liberty, was not only possible, but was in existence in Barcelona. 'Socialism', Orwell had recently written, 'is the only real enemy that Fascism has to face' (*RWP* 200). Now the fascist insurrection against the Spanish Republic had jolted Catalonia into revolution. A great inertia and defeatism had again and again prevented Orwell's fictional characters from changing their lives, and seemed to envelop England itself in a dull paralysis. But in Spain, in the crisis of civil war, something had shaken free, something had changed. And it seemed that the revolution itself was collectivized; it could belong to everyone.

The first thing that happens in *Homage to Catalonia* (1938) is an encounter, in the Lenin Barracks in Barcelona, the militia headquarters of the Partido Obrero de Unificación Marxista (POUM, the Workers' Party of Marxist Unification).[2] Orwell meets a young Italian militiaman, puzzling over a map on the officers' table. They exchange a few words in Spanish, and shake hands; they will never see each other again. It is one of those vivid, almost allegorical encounters with some other that punctuate Orwell's writing about his life. Whether or not it actually happened, or happened like that, the meeting is highly charged, crackling with ideological and personal significance. The handclasp represents entry into a community (Orwell was there to enlist), masculine like Orwell's other communities, but this time potentially utopian, a European community that binds together the Italian and the Englishman, the worker and the bourgeois, the illiterate and the writer. The image might be that of a propaganda poster – Peasants and Intellectuals Unite! – and arguably it is a patronizing one, with its observation that 'obviously' the uneducated Italian 'could not make head or tail of the map' (*HC* 1). (It is entirely characteristic of Orwell's style that the fluent declaration of solidarity is awkwardly interrupted by a stubborn reminder of practical inequality.) Orwell had not after all magically shed his old identity, or left behind him inherited attitudes to peasants, for example, or Mediterranean peoples, as some of his later remarks about the Spanish make clear. He could not change who he was but he could try to take action to change his relation with others, and that was the meaning of the handclasp with the Italian militiaman, who later became bound up for Orwell with all his memories of that period of the war, 'the red flags in Barcelona, the gaunt trains full of shabby soldiers creeping to the front, the grey war-stricken towns further up the line, the muddy, ice-cold trenches in the mountains' (*HC* 2).

Barcelona was a revelation, with its walls scrawled with the hammer and sickle, its demolished churches, and servile and even ceremonial forms of speech replaced by 'Comrade' and 'Salud!'. 'All this was queer and moving. There was much in it that I did not understand, in some ways I did not even like it, but I recognised it immediately as a state of affairs worth fighting for' (*HC* 3). As once before in the rue du Coq d'Or, a European scene seemed to offer the chance of a different way of life. And if Spain was a political education, it was an emotional one too. *Down and Out* is an emotionally reticent, even inhibited book, with a narrator who sometimes seems to want to hide behind the furniture of its colourful or grim detail. Reticence and inhibition were the climate of Orwell's upbringing, a climate carried over into his first novel of English life, with its well-brought-up and self-effacing heroine. 'One of the effects of safe and civilised life is an immense over-sensitiveness which makes all the primary emotions seem somewhat disgusting,' he wrote in 1942. 'But in Spain we were not living in a normal time.' Consequently in Spain he had, and *shared*, a wealth of 'emotionally widening experience', which he saw as one of the by-products of revolution (*CW* xiii. 502). Undoubtedly his marriage to Eileen O'Shaughnessy, who came with him to Barcelona, was part of this education in feeling and expression. He became less painfully inhibited by his own ill-fitting incongruity, and this helped him to write more plainly – for there is an emotional as well as a political dimension to his assertion, in 'Inside the Whale' (1940), that 'good novels are written by people who are *not frightened*' (*CW*

xii. 106). He had certainly not belonged in Wigan; the second part of *The Road to Wigan Pier* is his long apology for being there. He did not belong in Spain either, but he knew he was in the right place. And so he did not feel it was naive to open *Homage to Catalonia* with the encounter with the Italian militiaman, a sort of heraldic emblem of comradeship that explained what Orwell was doing there. It was simple, as he remembered it later. 'In spite of power politics and journalistic lying, the central issue of the war was the attempt of people like this to win the decent life which they knew to be their birthright' (*CW* xiii. 509). 'I never saw the Italian militiaman again,' he added, 'nor did I ever learn his name. It can be taken as quite certain that he is dead' (*CW* xiii. 510).[3]

With the country divided by civil war, political life in the different regions of Spain was taking different forms. In Catalonia, and its chief city Barcelona, the anarchists were virtually in control at the time Orwell and his wife arrived, and were raising troops of militia to defend the Republic. Orwell joined the militia of the POUM (and Eileen worked in the POUM offices) because of the POUM's association with the Independent Labour Party in Britain, and he was soon training in the Lenin Barracks with this ill-assorted, under-equipped, and politically conscious rag-tag army of volunteers. No doubt his own experience in the disciplined services in Burma was useful, but the militia was a very different, virtually opposite sort of force from the Burma police. It was an organization based on a system of social equality between officers and men. Every soldier drew the same pay, regardless of rank, and lived under the same conditions. Officers were elected, and military life was punctuated by 'those enormous arguments by means of which discipline is gradually hammered out in revolutionary armies' (*CW* xiii. 502). It seems remarkable that it worked at all. But by most accounts the anarchist militias were capable fighting forces, and morale was extremely high.

The book is Orwell's homage to Catalonia (not to Spain), but the front-line service that he saw was on the Aragón front, first in the mountains near Alcubierre, and later in hills to the east of Huesca, which the government troops were besieging. Alcubierre was in a quiet sector, which was just as well, since at first Orwell's *centuria* had no rifles. They looked like a rabble

– eighty men and several dogs – as they shambled up to the front line. Orwell does not idealize the Spanish militiamen among whom he lived, nor his relation with them, but he describes them with tenderness. This derives from their open friendliness and in part from his knowledge of what was to become of most of them, and perhaps too from the example of the preceding generation of poets and memoirists of the First World War, like Wilfred Owen and Siegfried Sassoon, whose work is such a powerful presence in English writing in the 1930s. Still, he writes, of course, as a foreigner, and a bourgeois. In his eyes the Spanish are warm, friendly, and generous, but exasperatingly vague and undependable. As an Englishman who first learned about foreigners in the colonial East, he is apt to think of the Spanish as a little insufficient, even childish. This impression was certainly reinforced by the fact that at least half of his militia company were literally children, 16 years old at the very most. Aragón itself was underdeveloped, and trailed far behind the modernity of industrial countries. It was desperately impoverished and backward. Orwell describes his feeling of nausea at coming upon a harrow in a derelict hut in no man's land, an implement so primitive as to seem to belong to the Stone Age. He would never have thought of the French, for example, or the Germans, as immature, but the people of southern Europe, with their poverty, their superstitious religious practices, and their obscure squabbles, were the nearest thing to orientals in Europe, from the English point of view. As there are strangely few Burmese actually named in *Burmese Days*, so too there are not many speaking parts for the Spanish in *Homage to Catalonia*. But the modality of observation is quite different. Burma had been viewed in the novel, however sympathetically, through the eyes of the alienated and useless Flory. It had also shown itself incapable of doing anything about its state of abjection. But Spain had, at least at first, embraced the sympathetic foreigner, and enlisted him quite literally in the struggle for its freedom. Unlike the shadowy and ineffectual nationalist movement in *Burmese Days*, these Spanish forces were mounting a credible resistance to authoritarian oppression. And so the militia became an important symbol for Orwell – less as a fighting force, for relatively little actual fighting is reported in the book, than as a kind of ramshackle model society, both in its democratic organization and in its dedication to political ends he considered worth fighting for.

In *The Road to Wigan Pier* he had catalogued all the obstacles – political, economic, and psychological – that stood in the path of the achievement of socialism in England. On the streets of Barcelona, and now in the mountains of Aragón, the prevailing mental atmosphere actually was that of socialism, and he found himself, disconcertingly, in the majority.

> I had dropped more or less by chance into the only community of any size in Western Europe where political consciousness and disbelief in capitalism were more normal than their opposites. Up here in Aragón one was among tens of thousands of people, mainly though not entirely of working-class origin, all living at the same level and mingling on terms of equality. In theory it was perfect equality, and in practice it was not far from it. (*HC* 83)

Ordinary class divisions had disappeared, he went on, to an extent unthinkable in 'the money-tainted air of England'. This state was possible, of course, partly because of the absence of any ordinary economic life among the militia. (When Orwell is wounded, the first thing his comrades do after carrying him to safety is to make off with all his portable possessions, his watch and revolver and torch and knife: to each according to his need.) In *The Road to Wigan Pier*, he had identified everyday speech as the great sustainer of class division and antagonism in England. But the POUM militia contained an anarchic mixture of nationalities and languages, and meanwhile Orwell's command of Spanish was confined to rudimentary communication, making him and his interlocutors deaf to the inflections of class and provenance (and he does not seem to have learned any Catalan); so at least to his ear there was no equivalent to the layering of prestige that poisoned speech in England. And so the story here, for once, was one of integration and a sense of belonging. In spite of the cold and the dirt, the relentless boredom and the occasional terror, it is a story of the kind of happiness that comes from being in the right place.

Though the setting was most unlikely, Orwell's account of the Aragón front has some of the classic ingredients of a pastoral idyll – the rural, indeed shepherdly landscape, the simplicity of the life, the comradeship among men, the fact that nothing much happens most of the time, and even the occasional tragic death. But it did not last, being in the end overwhelmed by idyll's great adversary, history. Returning to Barcelona after five months at the front, Orwell could soon see how much things had changed in the city. Signs of social division had begun to reappear in the streets. The government-controlled Popular Army was establishing control and the militia were beginning to be discredited. The political alliance that had made the 1936 revolution was coming to pieces: Orwell's account of it bristles with mutually hostile acronyms. He finds himself caught up in street fighting between the anarchist groups on one side and the police and Assault Guards on the other. This nasty, confusing, and dangerous episode is brought to an end with the arrival of government troops from Valencia, but the 'horrible atmosphere of suspicion and hostility' continues (*HC* 126). Though nobody is really sure what is going on at the time, it becomes clear that for the Valencia Government, now taking its lead from the communists, this is an opportunity to assume fuller control over Catalonia, and especially over the anarchist forces. What was to follow, in May and June, has been described as 'the Stalinisation of Barcelona',[4] as the communists set about suppressing the revolutionary parties. In due course the POUM is charged with being a secret fascist organization, 'Franco's fifth column', and outlawed, almost all its leaders disappearing into prisons. The workers' militias are broken up and redistributed among the Popular Army. All the joyous volubility Orwell had marvelled at a few months before is gone; orthodoxy is the enemy of dialogue, and only the party line can raise its voice. The anarchist press in Catalonia is censored while the communist papers denounce the POUM as Trotskyist crypto-fascists. It is just the kind of twentieth-century story we have come to think of as Orwellian.

Under orders from his Belgian company commander and friend Georges Kopp (who was later to be imprisoned), Orwell spent most of the days of the Barcelona fighting in May on a rooftop, ready to defend the POUM buildings on the other side of the street from attack by the Assault Guards. It was the roof of an observatory over a museum over a cinematograph (the ideal vantage for watching history take its course), and Orwell says he would sit on the roof marvelling at the folly of it all. For what he was watching was not a defeat but a betrayal, or rather the first phase of a betrayal. The Catalonian revolution was being assaulted not by Franco's forces, still less by German or Italian fascists, but by Catalonian revolutionaries.

In the uneasy peace that followed the street fighting, Orwell's leave came to an end and he returned to the front, to be almost immediately wounded, shot in the throat, and then evacuated to a series of clearing stations and hospitals. When he made his way back to Barcelona he knew nothing of recent events there, and he describes how he ambled into the lounge of the Hotel Continental quite unaware that the POUM had just been suppressed and the police were arresting everyone they could find who had any connection to it. Four hundred or more people were immediately arrested in Barcelona alone, and in the months that followed the number of political prisoners, not counting fascists, swelled into thousands. Orwell was not a party member of the POUM but he was at risk as a POUM militiaman. He found himself again down and out, sleeping in the streets to avoid arrest, for houses known to harbour POUM supporters were under observation, and hotels and boarding houses had to inform police of new arrivals. During the day, incongruously enough, it was safe enough for Orwell and his friends to walk the streets in the guise of prosperous English visitors. The purge was at first kept out of the Barcelona press, and – a particular bitterness – men at the front in the anarchist militias knew nothing about it. This was just at the time when the bloody attack on Huesca was beginning. 'In the intervening days there must have been numbers of men who were killed without ever learning that the newspapers in the rear were calling them Fascists' (*HC* 162). As in *Animal Farm*, the indignation is sharpened by the irony.

One effect of all this on Orwell was to recall his Englishness. Having identified himself with a European cause, he now recognizes that it has gone wrong in a way that would not (or not yet) be possible in England. In England, he says, though there is political persecution in a petty way, there is a tradition of political mildness that stands in the way of the extremism and thuggery that have come to seem natural in the nightmare atmosphere of Barcelona (*HC* 151). Having done all he can to help the imprisoned Kopp, and being himself in constant danger of arrest, all he wants now is to get out of Spain, and this he and his wife and another proscribed friend manage to do, again ironically, by crossing the frontier in the dining car of a train where they are unchallenged because they look like respectable middle-class foreigners. The revulsion from the foreign, and grateful relapse into a comfortable Englishness, is a familiar enough motif in a certain kind of travel writing (and travel), but in Orwell's case here it is unillusioned. If England is too solid and respectable to succumb to the fate of Barcelona, at least for the time being, it is also too solid and respectable to understand it, and this could be a fatal weakness. Orwell recalls how he himself found it hard to take the danger entirely seriously. 'The whole thing seemed too absurd. I had the ineradicable English belief that "they" cannot arrest you unless you have broken the law. It is a most dangerous belief to have during a political pogrom' (*HC* 181). And so the return to England, with which *Homage to Catalonia* closes, is in equal measure a return to Eden and to cloud cuckoo land. He and his wife are haunted – thinking, talking, and dreaming incessantly of Spain. But England knows nothing of these things; after all, it is the English and not the Spanish who have not grown up.

> Down here it was still the England I had known in my childhood: the railway-cuttings smothered in wild flowers, the deep meadows where the great shining horses browse and meditate, the slow-moving streams bordered by willows, the green bosoms of the elms, the larkspurs in the cottage gardens; and then the huge peaceful wilderness of outer London, the barges on the miry river, the familiar streets, the posters telling of cricket matches and Royal weddings, the men in bowler hats, the pigeons in Trafalgar Square, the red buses, the blue policemen – all sleeping the deep, deep sleep of England, from which I sometimes fear that we shall never wake till we are jerked out of it by the roar of bombs. (*HC* 187)

It is another Orwellian list, evoking a maternal landscape in comfy rhythms strikingly different of course from the catalogues evocative of Spain – 'air raids, trenches, machine guns, screaming trams, milkless tea . . .' (*HC* 153). Its landscape is that of George Bowling's Lower Binfield, and so perhaps is the explosive fate that awaits it, for it is an England fast asleep, dreaming that it is an island.

This sleepy and innocent-seeming panorama of England is the same as the 'wide prospect' contemplated by Clover, the stout motherly carthorse in *Animal Farm* (1945), in her bewilderment just after the show trials in the farmyard in which various animals have had their throats ripped out on the orders of the dictator Napoleon (*AF* 58). *Animal Farm* is a European book in three dimensions. Its imagery is entirely English, and homely in an intimate sense. Orwell said that, when he was a child, most middle-class boys grew up within sight of a farm (*CW* xii. 93), and they all had model farmyard animals in the toy box. The scene of the story was immediately recognizable in a thoroughly English idiom, and so were its animal characters or stereotypes like the patient carthorse, the contrary donkey, the greedy pigs. But the story itself was made in Russia. 'Please say that A.F. is intended as a satire on dictatorship in general,' Orwell instructed his literary agent in 1947, 'but *of course* the Russian Revolution is the chief target. It is humbug to pretend anything else' (*CW* xix. 234). The story of the revolt in the farmyard shadows Soviet history ingeniously, not just in outline with the pigs Napoleon and Snowball corresponding to the rivals Stalin and Trotsky, but in its careful parallels with such events as the naval mutiny at Kronstadt and the Treaty of Rapallo. The third dimension of the book is Spanish, because its theme is the betrayal of revolution and it was in Barcelona that Orwell had seen this happen at close quarters.

His own experience of the Stalinist suppression and purge of the anarchists in Catalonia provided the emotional force of *Animal Farm*, making it Orwell's most moving book. The preface he wrote in 1947 for the Ukrainian edition of the book spells out just how vital that Spanish experience was as a motive for *Animal Farm*. (The translation was made for the benefit of Ukrainians, former Bolsheviks but later inmates of Siberian prison camps, living in Displaced Persons Camps in Germany after the war. The 5,000 copies of the Ukrainian edition never reached the people for whom they were intended, because they were intercepted by the American Military Government in Munich and handed over to the Soviet Repatriation Commission, who presumably knew what to do with them.[5])

Many of his friends, he explains, were among those hunted down in Barcelona as Trotskyists, and imprisoned or murdered; these manhunts coincided with the great Stalinist purges and show trials in the USSR and were a sort of supplement to them. When Orwell and his wife returned from Spain to England, they found many sensible and well-informed observers 'believing the most fantastic accounts of conspiracy, treachery and sabotage which the press reported from the Moscow trials' (*CW* xix. 87). The story of *Animal Farm* allegorizes the history of the Soviet Revolution, but its fury derives from Spain. And its setting in the rural heartland of the English imagination is designed to bring the story home to a people whose own history gave them no real understanding of things like concentration camps, mass deportations, arrests without trial, or press censorship. In England the 'soft-boiled emancipated middle class' in particular were enthusiastic about Russia out of ignorance, Orwell said, and could 'swallow totalitarianism because they have no experience of anything except liberalism' (*CW* xii. 103). Further, since Hitler's invasion of Russia in 1941, Stalin had become overnight a war ally and potential saviour of Europe, 'this disgusting murderer', as Orwell called him (*CW* xii. 522), embraced by the British press and public as the heroic and even lovable 'Uncle Joe'.

The betrayal in Barcelona had not only been murderous. It had also been accompanied, like the larger purges in Russia, by a great propaganda offensive designed to justify and disguise what had taken place. So pervasive and meretricious was the barrage of lies that Orwell was inclined to believe that an objective history of even the facts of the Spanish Civil War (or anything else) might henceforth be impossible. This is a theme that bulks very large in *Nineteen Eighty-Four*, but it is present already in *Animal Farm*. When Squealer, the pig who is Napoleon's spin doctor, reveals to the astonished animals that Snowball has all along been in league with the enemy, he announces in the classic Stalinist fashion that this has all been proved 'by documents which he left behind him and which we have only just discovered' (*AF* 53). Within the constraints of its fairly simple framework, *Animal Farm* has quite a lot to say about the corruption of language. To begin with, and like all revolutions, the animals' revolt is excitedly talkative. It takes its inspiration from the prophetic words of the patriarchal old pig Major, who bequeaths to the others gifts of language, a utopian dream, a revolutionary anthem, and a stirring speech. The themes of his speech are liberation, equality, and comradeship among animals, the equivalent to the simple statement of socialist ideals called for towards the end of *The Road to Wigan Pier*. These revolutionary ideals become codified by the clever pigs into an ideology, Animalism, expressed in the form of the Seven Commandments of the revolution (actually three principles and four prohibitions), which are painted on the side of the barn wall (*AF* 15). The betrayal of the revolution can thereafter be exactly measured – though not by the animals themselves, and this is very much the point – in the modification, compromise, abandonment, or direct reversal of these commandments. This is a process that starts to happen almost immediately, with Snowball's dumbing-down of the principles of Animalism, for the benefit of the stupider animals, to the slogan 'Four legs good, two legs bad'. After the overthrow of the farmer, Mr Jones, there are at first weekly meetings, instituting a form of participatory democracy in which every animal has a vote. These become the forum for the rivalry between Napoleon and Snowball, until Snowball is driven out and discredited and Napoleon becomes effectively a dictator. Napoleon has never had much taste for discussion, and his very first pronouncement after Snowball's defeat is that there will be no more debates; all matters of policy will be decided by a special committee of pigs meeting in private, and their decisions communicated to the others. This move deprives the other animals of a political voice, a 'say' in the process of government, which has now become monological and autocratic. And, since most of the other animals have difficulty reading (not to mention writing), and remembering, they are not well equipped to check the actions of the government against the precepts of the law, painted on the barn wall, which in any case seem unaccountably to keep changing.

Linguistically, therefore, they are reduced to the function of listening to the command of the dictator, mediated through his instruments of propaganda, and doing what they are told.

The traditional conceit on which the beast fable is founded is that animals can speak. Indeed they do continue to speak under Napoleon's regime (though they will be reduced to silence before the story ends), but their speech, never particularly eloquent or complex, is subject to discursive pressures that work to weaken what intellectual content it had. Squealer the state propagandist is particularly active in this, playing on the animals' sense of their own limited understanding and poor memory, in effect coaxing them to allow the state, embodied in Napoleon, to do their thinking for them. Prescribed speech options are provided for them, in the form of slogans to chant and songs to sing. Certainly Napoleon's regime is coercive, violent, and deadly. But it is also hegemonic, operating not just through a regime of terror but also through imposing a form of assent, controlling the animals' behaviour through its control of language and therefore its control, or prevention, of thought. This is familiar ground for Orwell, if we remember the wretched *plongeurs* in Paris, too exhausted to think and therefore deprived of agency, or even the disciples of the money god in *Keep the Aspidistra Flying*, mesmerized into conformity by a constant stream of mindless slogans. When the sheep are trained to bleat 'Four legs good, two legs bad!' – and later, with equal enthusiasm, 'Four legs good, two legs better!' – the purpose is not only to drown out others' voices but also to make speech itself mindless (a function to be performed in *Nineteen Eighty-Four* by Newspeak), and therefore to destroy the possibility of dissent. In his essay 'Politics and the English Language', published in *Horizon* in 1946, Orwell warned about the corrupting powers of orthodox language, and how, 'by simply throwing your mind open and letting the ready-made phrases come crowding in', it was possible (and tempting) to acquiesce in the invasion of your freedom of thought; and 'this reduced state of consciousness, if not indispensable, is at any rate favourable to political conformity' (*CW* xvii. 427). Totalitarian language takes this to brutal extremes, swallowing up individual speech. It is the black hole of discourse, transforming everything into itself. In

'The Prevention of Literature', Orwell showed he was inclined to believe that, under totalitarianism, literature itself, in as much as it has tended to be the vehicle of intellectual enquiry and a devotion to truth, would simply come to an end – not necessarily crushed by authority, but betrayed by a weakening of the desire for liberty among intellectuals themselves (*CW* xvii. 374). These are matters that go beyond the simple contours of *Animal Farm*, but there is enough about discourse and ideology in this book to prepare a reader for the further elaboration of these themes in *Nineteen Eighty-Four*. It is appropriate to add here the habitual refusal of the cynical donkey Benjamin to take part in political discourse at all, the antics of the state poet Minimus with his anthem 'Comrade Napoleon', and the sincere willingness of the animals for the most part to speak in the language that enslaves them. 'You would often hear one hen remark to another, "Under the guidance of our Leader, Comrade Napoleon, I have laid five eggs in six days" ' (*AF* 62).

Orwell rather inaccurately subtitled *Animal Farm* 'A Fairy Story', but there is nothing of the supernatural in it if you accept the basic premiss of the talking animals. It is a political satire in the form of a beast fable allegorizing the betrayal of the Russian Revolution, and, in the virtue of the simplicity of its idea, language, and design, it is the only one of his fictions that does not suffer from some important flaw. The implications of the story's animality, however, are not as simple as they may look. We have seen how, from *Down and Out* to *Homage to Catalonia*, Orwell's imagination was engaged with the plight of the victims of forms of injustice and cruelty. It is his major theme. We have also seen how he was not always sure how to represent such people, being particularly hampered by what seemed the ambiguity of his own location in relation to them, and how this often produced clumsinesses of style, expression, and attitude. In *Burmese Days*, for example, there is an indecision about how closely the narrative point of view is identified with the consciousness of Flory, compounded by an indecisiveness in Flory's own attitudes towards people around him in Burma, attributable to his mixed feelings and his possession of (and reaction against) cultural reflexes inherited from his class, education, and associates. Natives or proletarians, the unemployed in Wigan and Bradford or the illiterate boy soldiers in the Aragón trenches, even the depressed provincial spinster, Orwell tends to find himself observing such embattled people without being of them – coming rather, because of who he was, often from what might be thought of as the other side. And one result of this has been a tendency to think of them, in their predicament, as in some ways insufficient – childish, or innocent, unaware, inarticulate, unthinking, helpless, unevolved. Such characterizations also inscribe in his narratives the distance between observer and observed, and sometimes lay the observer open to a charge of being patronizing, or worse. In making the decision now to write a story that actually is about animals, Orwell is both acknowledging the old problem of how to represent others, and turning it to a kind of advantage, in what turn out to be quite subtle ways.

Animal Farm is a story in the ironic mode, giving its readers an understanding that is ahead of, and greater than, that of the characters. The representation of the pigs, and the human characters, is 'estranged' – that is to say, external and dramatic. We see what Napoleon and Snowball and Squealer do and say, but we never enter their minds and share their thoughts, as we do with other animals such as Boxer and Clover, and frequently in a sort of generalized access to something like public opinion on Animal Farm, what 'the animals' as a community thought and felt. However, the animals' thought processes are pretty limited. We watch Boxer, for example, struggling to get beyond the letter D in the alphabet.[6] Sometimes, the animals have to be helped with some such formula as 'If she could have spoken her thoughts, it would have been to say . . .', or 'If she herself had had any picture of the future, it had been . . .', and so on (*AF* 58). There is no Gulliver-like reporter in the scene. Instead, from the first chapter, in which we are given access to the secret beginnings of their revolt out of sight of their human masters, Orwell's impersonal narrator stays faithful to the experience and understanding of his animal characters, and the narrative remains lodged in their point of view. 'Out of spite, the human beings pretended not to believe that it was Snowball who had destroyed the windmill: they said it had fallen down because the walls were too thin' (*AF*

49). The modality of 'out of spite' and 'pretended' marks this as the opinion of the animals, and this is not contradicted or doubted. The narrator does not voice the sceptical question that the statement raises (perhaps the human beings were right?), which would put the questioner in odd complicity with the animals' sworn enemies; and he is similarly deadpan in reporting later developments. 'The animals now also learned that Snowball had never – as many of them had believed hitherto – received the order of "Animal Hero, First Class". This was merely a legend which had been spread some time after the Battle of the Cowshed by Snowball himself' (*AF* 65). It would take a very slow-witted reader to miss the fact that these bland assertions deny an event that has already been entered into the narrative record itself, in chapter four, so that the narrative is actually forgetting itself, and committing a scandalous self-contradiction. By this simple device, the work of ironic interpretation is devolved on the reader, and the reader's own intelligence and memory and scepticism are required to outreach the limited grasp of the animals and, apparently, of the observer who tells their story.

The narrator disingenuously keeps to the interpretative pace of the animals themselves. Naively believing the pigs to have all animals' interests at heart, Boxer and the rest are easy to dupe, and fatally slow to see how they are exploited and their revolution betrayed. But to read the book properly, we are bound to read it ironically, bringing to bear a human experience and expectation of selfishness, cruelty, and lies that enable us to see what is going on long before it becomes clear to the victims themselves. (The first danger sign was there at the end of chapter two.) So the more ironically – and therefore more successfully, and enjoyably – we read, the more we distance and estrange ourselves from the point of view of the poor dumb animals. Irony, a greater access to knowledge through an understanding that things and particularly words do not always mean what they seem to mean, sets us above the helplessly unironic animals. Indeed this sense of superiority is one of the pleasures of irony. Irony is one of the opposites of innocence. It is a quality and perhaps a consolation of fallen language, and a human faculty; animals are too stupid for it. But in the context of this story and its development, to identify oneself as a human being is ultimately to identify oneself as a pig. So, when we arrive knowingly at the end of the story, with our insider knowledge far in advance of the understanding of 'the animals outside' (*AF* 94), and perhaps exclaim to ourselves 'There, I knew it! The pigs have turned into human beings!', we may not always appreciate the alignment that the narrative has manœuvred us into, a sympathy with the victims but an unavoidable identification (by virtue of what we are, as readers) with the exploiters. It was a location familiar to Orwell, of course. He had been there for most of his life.

Animal Farm was finished early in 1944 but did not appear – after many rejections by other publishers, including Victor Gollancz, and T. S. Eliot at Faber & Faber – until August 1945, published by Secker & Warburg. Orwell travelled to France, Germany, and Austria in the spring of that year, as a correspondent for the *Manchester Evening News* and the *Observer*, and saw for himself the stricken face of Europe at the end of Hitler's war. 'To walk through the ruined cities of Germany is to feel an actual doubt about the continuity of civilization' (*CW* xvii. 122). In a post-war essay, 'Notes on Nationalism' (*CW* xvii. 141–57), he tried to analyse the psychological condition that had brought about the war and was now starting to inspire what he was the first to call the 'cold war' (*CW* xvii. 321). Nationalism was the habit of identifying oneself with a single nation or other unit, and placing it beyond good and evil; it was power hunger tempered by self-deception, a lethal, obsessive, and self-righteous fantasy. 'Nationalism' was not just about the nation. Orwell's sense of the word included 'such movements and tendencies as Communism, political Catholicism, Zionism, anti-Semitism, Trotskyism and Pacifism' (*CW* xvii. 142). A propensity to nationalism, to which everyone is subject, could be countered, if at all, only by 'discovering what one really is, what one's own feelings really are, and then . . . making allowance for the inevitable bias' (*CW* xvii. 155). That discovery was a process he himself had been struggling with for years. Meanwhile, the future for a post-war but not post-nationalist Europe looked grim. The Continent had almost fought itself to death, and emerged in 1945, shrunken and exhausted, between two highly militarized and ideologically self-righteous superstates, the Soviet Union and the United

States. If it became necessary to choose to subordinate British policy to that of one Great Power or the other, he wrote in 1947, 'everyone knows in his heart that we should choose America' (*CW* xix. 182). But even – perhaps especially – in its depressed and weakened state, Europe still stood for Orwell, as it always had, for the opportunity of a different and preferable way of life. 'Socialism does not exist anywhere, but even as an idea it is at present valid only in Europe. . . . Therefore a socialist United States of Europe seems to me the only worthwhile political objective today' (*CW* xix. 164). Returning to his perennial theme, he insisted that this could not begin to come about until Europeans had abandoned their overseas empires. It was not only communism that loomed over a vulnerable Europe. But it was in the end Europe that was the last hope, a location that could conceivably nurture a way of life different from the excesses of both its giant neighbours, and of its own past. There were European traditions and institutions that at least offered the possibility of social democracy, and 'Social Democracy, unlike capitalism, offers an alternative to communism' (*CW* xix. 181). Meanwhile, as the war was ending, and Europeans were beginning to see what life might be like in the cold war and the atomic age, Orwell had started to work on what was to be his final book. Its provisional title was *The Last Man in Europe*.

5

Oceania

A man called Winston Smith looks down at a labouring woman (*NEF* 228–9). He is a minor Party functionary in London, principal city of Airstrip One, a province of the superstate Oceania, and he is standing at the window of the room he has rented for clandestine meetings with his lover, who stands beside him. The woman below, a 'prole' about 50 years old, is hanging out washing on a line in the yard. She belongs to a class of people he would not normally notice, but she is singing a song as she works and it is the song that has attracted his attention. She is no beauty, this figure shapeless with childbearing and roughened by physical work. In fact to Winston she appears hardly human, with her 'mare-like' buttocks and skin coarse 'like an over-ripe turnip', and he supposes she has 'no mind', but only strong arms, a warm heart, and a fertile belly. But in an access of fellow feeling, he suddenly perceives her to be beautiful, in her strength, her courage, her suffering, and her teeming creativity. And she is an integral part of the natural scene, Winston's feeling for her being somehow romantically mixed up with the aspect of the sky above, that is the same for everyone. His thoughts become rhapsodic.

> And the people under the sky were also very much the same – everywhere, all over the world, hundreds of thousands of millions of people just like this, people ignorant of one another's existence, held apart by walls of hatred and lies, and yet almost exactly the same – people who had never learned to think but who were storing up in their hearts and bellies and muscles the power that would one day overturn the world. If there was hope, it lay in the proles! (*NEF* 229)

Here is another variation of that paradigm recognition scene that has its origins in Orwell's representations of the Orient, and we can also see how once again that moment of romantic kinship and identity gives way to a restoration of distance, an alienation. For by the end of this train of thought Winston is looking forward to a popular prole uprising that could not possibly include him, made by people 'who had never learned to think' and who would regard someone like him as an enemy, in the name of a future that would be just as alien to him as the hated present. And the next thing that happens is the brutal intrusion of the Thought Police, who smash into the room and wrench him away from this delusive idyll, incidentally doing injury or worse to the woman in the yard. And we next see Winston in the police cells beneath the Ministry of Love, where another enormous working-class woman, a drunken fellow-prisoner, vomits over him and declares sentimentally that she might be his mother. In the light of this cruel lesson in the realities of his predicament, should Winston's high-flown hymn to the working class be read ironically, the whole scene a cynical comment on the futility of his revolt against the Party and his sentimental delusion about people he knows nothing about? After all, by the end of *Nineteen Eighty-Four* there is absolutely no sign of political consciousness among the proletariat of Oceania. Winston's shortcomings – in his grasp of political theory, his social experience, and his emotional capacity – are no secret, and nor is the fact that there is no foreseeable way he or anyone else can overthrow the Party's tyranny in Oceania. But this does not necessarily invalidate Winston's intuition, that, if there *is* hope, it lies in the proles.

Orwell's own attitude to socialism at this time was akin to Gandhi's response when asked for his view of Western civilization (he is said to have replied that he thought it would be a very good idea). He had glimpsed socialism in Barcelona and the trenches of Aragón, and for a while in the early years of the war he thought he could see it coming in England. He did not see much of it in the programme of the Labour government under Attlee that swept to power in Britain in 1945; he considered these Labour reforms over-cautious and compromised, though it is proper to describe him as remaining a 'critical supporter' of the Attlee government.[1] He most emphatically did not find it either in the National Socialism of Hitler or in the union of Socialist Republics under Stalin. As he had argued in *The Road to Wigan Pier,* he believed that socialism would require a revolution, not least a psychological and cultural one, before it could be accomplished. Its underlying ideals were justice and liberty and its principal enemy, in England at least, was the poison of the class system and its associated mentalities. A genuine socialist government would institute widespread nationalization of banks, industries, transport, and public utilities, and introduce radical measures to provide a fairer distribution of wealth, and equal opportunities in education. (Orwell was to be particularly disappointed that the Attlee government failed to abolish private schooling, and his essay on the pernicious practices and effects of his own education at prep school, 'Such, Such Were the Joys', drafted in 1947, was part of his contribution to the debate on private education.) Furthermore, a genuinely socialist government would be internationalist in sympathy, and would recognize that an overseas empire was not compatible with its commitment to justice. This programme is set out in *The Lion and the Unicorn: Socialism and the English Genius,* written in February 1941 (*CW* xii. 391–434). There is no evidence that Orwell ever changed his mind about these aims and objectives, though changing circumstances changed his views about how, when, and whether they might be achieved. 'The real object of Socialism is human brotherhood,' he wrote at the end of 1943, adding, 'One often has to aim at objectives which one can only dimly see' (*CW* xvi. 42). When he reviewed his career in 'Why I Write', in 1946, he claimed to be the kind of writer for whom political motives were less important than egoistic, aesthetic, and historiographical ones. Nevertheless, everything he had written since his journey to Spain in 1936 had been written, he said, '*against* totalitarianism, and *for* democratic Socialism, as I understand it' (*CW* xviii. 319). He had already begun to write the book that would become *Nineteen Eighty-Four.*

In many quarters *Nineteen Eighty-Four* was (and sometimes still is) taken to be an attack on socialism. Orwell categorically denied this (*CW* xx. 135). The tyrannical Party that rules Oceania is called Ingsoc, or English Socialism, by the same logic whereby the torture chambers of the Thought Police are housed in the Ministry of Love. The perversion of language, and particularly of names, is one of the principal themes of the novel, and Orwell believed that socialism itself in his lifetime had been traduced, almost fatally, by what had been done in its name. Socialism does not seem to have been much discredited by the murderous activities of Hitler's National Socialist Party, who tended to be named Nazis or Fascists, and had nothing but open contempt for socialists in other countries. But the USSR under Stalin was a different matter, using an evangelically socialist public rhetoric, theoretically still committed to a world socialist revolution, and working through the Communist International (Comintern) to secure the support and loyalty of socialists everywhere. Since the Barcelona purges and the great show trials and liquidations in the USSR in 1937 and later, Orwell had had no illusions about Stalin, and his views did not change when Germany invaded Russia in 1941 and Stalin suddenly became an ally. 'This disgusting murderer is temporarily on our side,' he wrote in his diary, 'and so the purges, etc, are suddenly forgotten' (*CW* xii. 522). After Hitler's defeat in 1945 (just before *Nineteen Eighty-Four* was begun), Orwell thought of Stalin as socialism's worst enemy. 'Indeed, in my opinion, nothing has contributed so much to the corruption of the original idea of Socialism as the belief that Russia is a Socialist country and that every act of its rulers must be excused, if not imitated' (*CW* xix. 88).

So the main topical antagonist of *Nineteen Eighty-Four* is Stalinism, which outraged Orwell for three reasons in particular. One was its stamping on the possibilities of freedom and justice in the Soviet Union and later its Eastern European satellites. Another was its monumental mendacity and its cynical deployment of the name and language of socialism. The third was the slavish loyalty of radical left-wing intellectuals and journalists in Britain to a Stalinist party line (for example, in obediently calling for a 'people's peace' when Stalin became Hitler's ally in 1939, a tune that immediately changed to a call to arms for a 'people's war' when Russia was invaded).

The tragedy of socialism was that throughout Orwell's political lifetime it was associated with one of history's most repulsive tyrants. *Nineteen Eighty-Four* is a study of tyranny, and, although Stalin was tyranny's most spectacular living avatar, there was no shortage of other examples to draw on. Technological developments, especially in communications technology, had given governments the power to control the lives of their citizens far more completely than ever before, through surveillance, censorship, and indoctrination. Military and ideological aggression, and the frequent readiness of intellectual and political leaders to espouse totalitarian ideas, meant that people like the British could no longer assume that tyranny was something that happened to foreigners. Orwell laid the scene of *Nineteen Eighty-Four* in Britain, he said, 'in order to emphasise that the English-speaking races are not innately better than anyone else and that totalitarianism, if not fought against, could triumph anywhere' (*CW* xx. 135). If justice was indivisible and everybody's business, so too was tyranny. This was itself an article of socialist faith, which had led Orwell to sign up at the Lenin Barracks in Barcelona a decade before, and fight for democracy in a foreign land.

In fact *Nineteen Eighty-Four*'s Oceania has elements of a large number of the institutions Orwell thought of as tyrannical in practice or potential. There are similarities between the portrayal of Winston Smith and Orwell's self-portrait as a snivelling and dejected schoolboy at prep school, in 'Such, Such Were the Joys'. 'That was the pattern of school life – a continuous triumph of the strong over the weak' (*CW* xix. 378). The machinery of despotism was something Orwell had experienced, as a reluctant and compromised insider, in colonial Burma, and in Morocco he had observed someone else's empire and marvelled at the way France's African subjects seemed mesmerized into docile obedience by an image of masterly authority (*CW* xi. 420). In *The Lion and the Unicorn* he had likened his own country to a family with the wrong members in control (*CW* xii. 401), and the regime of Big Brother rests on a sort of perversion of family loyalties and hierarchies. *A Clergyman's Daughter* had already shown how the family could be the location for the most bleak and hopeless slavery. The most invulnerable tyrannies were not those dependent on compulsion and force, but the ones locked into place by the consent of their subjects – like Dorothy Hare, for example, incapable of disobeying or escaping her bullying father.

There is much of Orwell's Spanish experience in *Nineteen Eighty-Four*, as there is in *Animal Farm*. The atmosphere of secrecy and betrayal, the actual terror of arrest, disappearance, torture, forced confession, and the rest, was something he knew about from Barcelona in 1937. The General Secretary of the POUM, Andrés Nin, to give only the most notorious example, was kidnapped by Communist agents, held in a secret prison, and tortured to death in an unsuccessful attempt to get him to confess that he and his comrades were fascist agents.[2] Orwell's disgust at the propaganda that discredited the POUM, and the way this was reflected in the orthodox left-wing press in Britain, makes its way into the novel's account of the work of the Ministry of Truth. The idea that the past itself has no existence, other than as a story to be manipulated and changed at the will of the powerful, derives not from Nietszche but from Orwell's widespread reading of accounts of the Spanish war, many of which he knew to be grossly partial if not downright inventions (by both sides), which would make up the historical record of the conflict for those who knew no better. The very concept of objective truth seemed to be fading out of the world, he wrote in 'Looking Back on the Spanish War': 'I am willing to believe that history is for the most part inaccurate and biased, but what is peculiar to our own age is the abandonment of the idea that history *could* be truthfully written' (*CW* xiii. 504). It is an anxiety that would bear fruit in the 'memory hole', and Winston's job rewriting history, in obedience to instructions like 'times 3.12.83 reporting bb dayorder doubleplusungood refs unpersons rewrite fullwise upsub antefiling' (*NEF* 46). Meanwhile, Orwell himself had had three dispiriting years in the business of propaganda and information management at the BBC, and his memories of the corporation, and the Ministry of Information to which it was answerable, were also to leave their traces on his imagination of Oceania (employees of the BBC today claim to recognize the Ministry of Truth canteen and, less plausibly, the food served there).

Winston Smith's London evokes the life of the wartime capital in a general way, with its permanent exhaustion, its rumours and shortages and discomforts and dangers, its curtailments of freedom, and its weak sense of the future. Above all, Oceanian London is a city under a bombardment of coercive discourse, with the ubiquitous face of Big Brother gazing down 'from every commanding corner' (*NEF* 4) – BIG BROTHER IS WATCHING YOU – and the three slogans of the Party, the propaganda films, the Two Minutes Hate, the bullying telescreen, and the way everyone's everyday speech is saturated with orthodox political sentiments. Perhaps the most interesting precedent for all this is the world of Gordon Comstock, in *Keep the Aspidistra Flying*, where the irresistible power of the New Albion advertising agency – itself a vision of a future England, as the name tells you – expressing itself in lobotomizing slogans and gigantic posters featuring the face of Roland Butta or Corner Table, succeeds in crushing individualism and dissent, and subjecting the whole world to the uniformity of consumption and the money god. Orwell's models of coercion were not only totalitarian political ideologies. The 'freedom' of the market too could produce a kind of slavery.

And so, although there is no sense in which Orwell thought of *Nineteen Eighty-Four* as in any way summative or conclusive, it does contain as much of his intellectual autobiography as *The Road to Wigan Pier*, as well as being a compendium of preoccupations from his earlier writings. Of the several political models on which Oceania is based, it is worth saying a little more here about that of the British colonialism with which the young Orwell had been involved, since it has been part of my argument to suggest that this remained a crucial paradigm in Orwell's political imagination. Orwell – or rather Goldstein, in 'the Book' which Winston reads in part two of the novel – is careful to say that the people of Oceania do not *feel* like a colonial population ruled from a distant capital. Oceania has no capital, no centre for a colonial periphery to aspire to or rebel against. Further, members of its ruling class are in theory selected on merit, and not on the basis of race or provenance. Even so, there are indications that it was in Burma that Orwell had first started to learn about Oceania.

Oceanian society is a caste system, comprising three strata – the Inner Party, the Outer Party, and the proles – with less flexibility and movement between the groups than in the class structure under capitalism (*NEF* 217–18). The governing group does not breed its successors but nominates them, and perpetuates its rule by sustaining its prestige and mystique in the eyes of the subject people. The Inner Party may protect its interests by occasionally allowing ambitious members of the Outer Party to rise (as U Po Kyin the Divisional Magistrate in Kyauktada was elected to the Club), while the bulk of the population, the proles, are kept in harmless subjection, uneducated and politically unconscious, living what is in effect an animal existence. Party members speak of the proles in dehumanizing and actually bestializing terms. 'The proles are not human beings,' says Winston's friend Syme 'carelessly' (*NEF* 56), stating what is obviously obvious to Party members, who never associate with them, and live and work in areas segregated from them. When Winston goes to a pub and gets into conversation with an aged prole, he is doing something eccentric and rather risky. For most people like him, the proles are as good as invisible, and beneath even contempt. This demeaning of a whole population by a privileged and powerful minority was a phenomenon Orwell had written about in *Burmese Days*. The proles, like the local population in Burma, are thought of by their masters as having no mental life. They live the life of the body, and the attitude of the party to the life of the body is indicated in the insane idealism of O'Brien, and in his vision of the future, in which the helpless body is exposed to endless violation by power exercised for its own sake – 'imagine a boot stamping on a human face – for ever' (*NEF* 280). This denial and underestimation of the humanity of most people was in Orwell's opinion the fatal flaw of imperialism, and it gives what strength there is to Winston's intuition that, if there is hope in Oceania, it lies in the proles.

The activity and orthodoxy of Party members is closely scrutinized, though there may be a large number of functionaries – the Brotherhood – who are secretly opposed to the system they serve, as Orwell thought there were in British India. But, since the proles offer little serious threat, they are allowed to get on with their low lives without much interference, and have a culture and speech that seem a good deal more expressive and lively than those of the ruling caste. They are, however, without political agency, completely excluded from the political process, and are consequently dehistoricized, living in something like a state of nature. Their rulers have their own high-status official language, Newspeak, a resource to which the proles have no access. In colonial Burma, inevitably, some local people could speak English, though the English-educated Veraswami was an object of especial scorn to Ellis, who also ranted at the Burmese butler in the Club for speaking English too well (*BD* 23). In Oceania, the linguistic boundaries are sharper. The intermediary caste in Oceania – for there is perhaps as much of Veraswami as of Flory in the status of Winston Smith and his Outer Party colleagues – are either happily acquiescent with the interest of the rulers on high, overwhelmed by their official role and its corresponding status, or, if in some way dissident, hampered by their alienation from the mass of the people. Meanwhile, the loyalty of the subjects of Oceania to their masters is sealed by constant reminders that their country is engaged in a war to the death with a sinister enemy, a persuasive ploy that was certainly familiar to the former BBC producer of wartime broadcasts to the King-Emperor's subjects in India.

And if Oceania has features of many extant forms of tyranny, it is also, of course, an imaginative projection of what might be to come. It is, however, a hypothesis rather than a prophecy. 'I do not believe that the kind of society I describe necessarily *will* arrive,' Orwell explained, 'but I believe (allowing of course for the fact that the book is a satire) that something resembling it *could* arrive' (*CW* xx. 135). He had before him the example of disturbing imaginary futures in the romances of H. G. Wells and the dystopias of Yevgeny Zamyatin's *We* and Aldous Huxley's *Brave New World*. A more prosaic projection was to be found in the work of the American political writer (and former Trotskyist) James Burnham, who claimed in *The Managerial Revolution* (1941) that capitalism was losing its power and would be replaced not by socialism but by the rule of a self-perpetuating administrative caste. Burnham also predicted the establishment of three rival managerial superstates, a geopolitics that would be reproduced in Orwell's Oceania, Eurasia, and Eastasia. In *The Struggle for the World* (1947) Burnham had shifted his ground. Managerialism was now associated specifically with the USSR. With the defeat of Germany and Japan, Burnham urged Americans to recognize that the 'Third World War' had already begun, pitting Western society against expansionist Soviet managerialism. Communists in the United States should be locked up without delay. The Soviet Union was bent on world domination, and America could counter this only by assuming the leadership of a global political world order – in effect establishing its own world empire, taking advantage (Burnham is a bit euphemistic about this) of its temporary monopoly on atomic weapons. ' "Power politics" is the only kind of politics there is'.[3] In a long review of this book (*CW* xix. 96–105), written while he was working on *Nineteen Eighty-Four*, Orwell expressed the hope that a socialist Europe might emerge as an alternative, in effect a counter-discourse to both the dangerous antagonists of this global shouting match. But it is worth noting that he also believed Burnham was wrong in his analysis and prediction, and this was in part because, in Orwell's opinion, Burnham over-rated the role played in human affairs by sheer force. Orwell did not think it was true that power politics is the only kind of politics there is. Burnham himself had succumbed, in the name of a kind of 'realism' that Orwell thought was particularly seductive to intellectuals, to the glamour of power. 'Power-worship blurs political judgement because it leads, almost unavoidably, to the belief that present trends will continue' (*CW* xviii. 278). The thuggish future represented in *Nineteen Eighty-Four*, and the future represented within the story by O'Brien's image of a boot stamping on a human face forever, is not Orwell's prediction of things to come. He had done enough prediction in his wartime writing, and had seen almost all of it prove to be wrong, to have lapsed into the humiliating but perhaps encouraging opinion that the future was unpredictable. *Nineteen Eighty-Four* is not a prophecy. It is something more like a dream.

This quality of the story is obscured by the fact that it looks just like a realist novel. Though it begins with the disorienting defamiliarization of the clocks striking thirteen, the novel goes on to evoke a very recognizable London, the shabby and run-down city of Gordon Comstock, made more depressing by the dangers and anxieties of wartime and the rationed austerities of the post-war years. As usual Orwell pays close attention to realizing the physical qualities of Winston Smith's life – his varicose ulcer, his breathlessness and tiredness, and the incidental trials, like the blocked drains and the loosely packed cigarette tobacco and the demoralizing canteen food, that make his life undignified and drab. There is a stronger sense of physical life here than in any of Orwell's books since *Down and Out*, and it is a life lived out amid the meticulously observed imagery of London in the 1940s, with almost none of the technological embellishments that might characterize this vision of the future as 'science fiction'. It is an almost too familiar world, and Winston himself is in the mould of the Orwellian protagonist, an antiheroic middle-class figure out of sympathy with the society and institutions he inhabits, making a weak and ineffectual attempt to escape or overturn them. All the first part of the novel establishes this world and beds it down in a credible everyday reality – Winston at home, at work, with the neighbours, with colleagues, Winston wandering the streets; his memories, his sexual history, his secret non-conformity. So thoroughly is this work done, and so confidently do we come to inhabit the mind and perceptions of Winston Smith, through whose experience Oceania is made known to us, that this defuses some of the narrative hyperbole that follows.

But hyperbolic it is. Consider, for example, the credibility, in realist terms, of the refuge Winston finds in the room above Mr Charrington's shop, so conveniently available for his illicit assignations with Julia, with its kindly proprietor so understanding about the need for privacy. When Winston and Julia are arrested in the room over the shop, it turns out that the benign elderly Mr Charrington was all along a senior officer of the Thought Police, and is revealed to be in reality a sharp-featured man in his mid-thirties. 'He was still recognisable, but he was not the same person any longer' (*NEF* 233). It seems unlikely on the face of it that he could have been stationed permanently in disguise in a junk shop in a prole quarter, in the hope of entrapping passing Outer Party dissidents. It is coincidental, though not incredible, that Winston's only named colleagues from work, Syme and Parsons and Ampleforth, all fall foul of the Thought Police as he and Julia do. What does seem incompatible with a realist mode of representation is the incredibly elaborate attention lavished on Winston by the Party; the complicated entrapment; the extended interrogation over several months of this minor functionary by a senior member of the Inner Party; and O'Brien's extraordinary statement that Winston has been under his personal surveillance for seven years (*NEF* 256) – that is, since long before Winston's dissidence was known even to himself.

The Party itself is hyperbolical and grotesque. Modern history must make us cautious of describing any imagined act of folly or barbarism as incredible, but nevertheless what the Party exercises in Oceania is a sort of dream tyranny. It is not realistic in the way the description of Victory Mansions, or Winston's thought processes, are in the idiom of literary realism. O'Brien's claims to be able to override mathematics and gravity – the laws of nature – are not presented as the ravings of a deranged individual but the metaphysical basis of Party ideology, yet they are no more realistic than the research project to extract sunshine from cucumbers witnessed by Gulliver on his travels in Lagado. The great undertaking of Newspeak itself, involving the murder of politically incorrect vocabulary and the reduction of the language to a limited lexicon that would make unorthodoxy literally unthinkable, is a brilliant extrapolation of the party-line tendencies Orwell warned against in 'Politics and the English Language'. But we should not assume that he thought of it as a policy that could ever be put into practice, any more than we assume that he believed that two and two make five, or that the sun and stars revolve round the earth as O'Brien says they do (*NEF* 278). Oceania's language engineers expect Newspeak to have finally superseded Standard English by the year 2050. But languages in use are languages in motion, and, while it is possible to outlaw a language, this is not the same thing as destroying *meanings*, which are a potential not of a language but of language-users;[4] and meanwhile to exercise over everybody's daily usage the kind of total control the Party would require to keep Newspeak completely and forever orthodox is a task that would make the occasional wholesale rewriting of the historical record seem a trivial matter.

There is an extremism, a feverishness, about *Nineteen Eighty-Four* that bathes the whole story in a grotesque and dreamlike light, although it is furnished throughout with prosaic, even naturalistic imagery. The hyperbole of its realization extends too to the portrayal of the affair that develops between the unprepossessing Winston and Julia, the most improbable of office romances. Most readers will concur that this aspect of the novel stretches credibility. Julia herself – apparently virginal, actually sluttish and sexually enthusiastic – is, as feminist critics have complained, less a realistic character than a fantasy woman, who does indeed appear in Winston's dreams before they ever meet. Their first rendezvous takes place in an idyllic country setting that he has also dreamed about. There is a similar overdetermination in Winston's dreams of O'Brien and his promise that they will meet again in the place where there is no darkness. The prominence of dreams in the story gives, as it often does, a rough but reliable index of its overflowing the dimensions of realism. It seems only appropriate that the gormlessly orthodox Parsons should be denounced and arrested for having been dissident in his sleep (*NEF* 245). London, Airstrip One, may look like London, England, but it is no more an actual place than Animal Farm, and *Nineteen Eighty-Four* is, as Orwell himself called it, a satire.

Nineteen Eighty-Four then is poetic rather than realist in conception, though Oceania is contained in no framing device like an exotic journey (Gulliver leaving the familiar world at the start of his travels and returning for good at the end) or a dream (Alice falling asleep in the first chapter and waking from Wonderland in the last) or even the defamiliarizing animal-fable convention of *Animal Farm*. Its poetic and satirical hyperbole is a trope that removes Oceania from the actual and contemporary, and this has the effect, as in *Animal Farm*, of releasing Orwell from the besetting awkwardness of location, deriving from his social and political provenance, that had characterized his earlier work. He has no predetermined locus in Oceania, as he had had in colonial Burma and bourgeois England and even as a foreigner in embattled Spain. There is a trace of Orwell's compromised location, as we have seen, in Winston Smith's belief in a future proletarian revolution that would have no place for him. But in general Winston's place in the political environment is a simple one. He is one of its numberless victims. The Party is unambiguously hateful,

Winston seems to derive no benefit from his membership of Ingsoc, and he certainly feels no loyalty to it. Orwell shows no more affection for Winston than he does for his other main characters, or for his portrayals of his earlier selves. But there is nothing ambiguous about his representation of Winston's predicament.

The Party's rule over Oceania is a complete totalitarian regime, an absolute tyranny with no redeeming features or moments. As a matter of fact there are not many police in Oceania, but this is because there is no law to police, and the Party has no need to control people's actions if it can control their thoughts and their reality. It exercises a discourse tyranny, and does not really need to dictate behaviour or even command territory or resources so long as it has control over how its citizens perceive the world. This is why, although Winston could have been liquidated when or before he had his first dissident thought, O'Brien instead spends painstaking months (apparently) persuading him voluntarily to obey and even love Big Brother. This done, his inevitable execution later is of so little consequence that the story ends without waiting for it to happen. Dictating discourse, the Party can dictate reality as people experience it. From this, everything else follows – the absolute domination of nature, the power to change not just the historical record but the past as people remember it, and so on. And, while the Party's rule is a terror, it is also a hegemony, securing the complicity of its non-prole citizens (the proles do not matter to it) through doublethink:

> to know and not to know, to be conscious of complete truthfulness while telling carefully-constructed lies, to hold simultaneously two opinions which cancelled out, knowing them to be contradictory and believing in both of them; to use logic against logic, to repudiate morality while laying claim to it, to believe that democracy was impossible and that the Party was the guardian of democracy; to forget whatever it was necessary to forget, then to draw it back into memory again at the moment when it was needed, and then promptly to forget it again: and above all, to apply the same process to the process itself. (*NEF* 37)[5]

Where, then, is Orwell's location in all this? Is there an equivalent to the ideological counterpoint audible in the irony of *Animal Farm*? The narrative point of view of *Nineteen Eighty-Four* remains committed to Winston Smith's perceptions, seeing, remembering, understanding, and misunderstanding his experience as he does, at his pace. But Winston, even in his own estimation, is a poor specimen, isolated, and offering a token and short-lived resistance. It is not unusual to see *Nineteen Eighty-Four* written off as a depressed and defeatist statement, evidence of Orwell's complete political disillusionment and perhaps of the miseries of his terminal illness. It would be quite wrong to underestimate Orwell's political fears, personal difficulties, and physical suffering in these last years of his life. But it is important also to do justice to his courage, his continuing political faith, and his literary resourcefulness in *Nineteen Eighty-Four*. What stands against the novel's remorseless portrayal of the extremes of injustice and inhumanity is the novel itself.

A pattern emerges when we start to consider the things that are anathema to the rule of the Party in Oceania. Winston's first act of rebellion is an act of writing – specifically of handwriting. He begins to write in his diary, although he is reasonably certain that, if detected, which of course it will be, this is a transgression punishable by death. There are two almost tautologically related reasons for this. First, the Party cannot tolerate any unsupervised, unpredictable, and potentially unorthodox use of language. It aspires to be a completely monologic regime, one that controls not only everything that is said and written, but everything that *can* be said and written. The use of language for a private individual purpose – and a diary is the most private writing of all – cannot be countenanced because it violates the totality of this discourse totalitarianism. Winston's second and related crime derives from the fact that he keeps the diary, necessarily, in secret, writing it in a shallow alcove in his living room invisible to the prying telescreen. In the alcove, and in the diary, Winston has staked out a private space where an exiguous private life can be sustained. This private space finds a later and even riskier location in the room above Mr Charrington's shop where Winston has his assignations with Julia. The assertion of private space is an act of political rebellion in itself, since it claims a sphere of existence over which political authority has no rights. The last private space is within the skull, and indeed it is in Winston's subjectivity that the narrative spends most of its time, though Winston and Julia are proved wrong in their liberal supposition – 'They can't get inside you' (*NEF* 174) – that this last stronghold is inviolable. ('The secret freedom which you can supposedly enjoy under a despotic government is nonsense, because your thoughts are never entirely your own,' Orwell had written in 1944. 'It is almost impossible to think without talking. . . . Take away freedom of speech, and the creative faculties dry up' (*CW* xvi. 172–3).)

Julia too, as Winston recognizes, literally embodies ideological resistance. Her attractiveness and courage, her frank enjoyment of sex and other physical pleasures (like chocolate), her espousal of the pragmatism of the flesh – these are qualities that may be taken to confirm Orwell's disappointing view of women, but they are also all dangerously subversive in the eyes of the Party. Indeed Julia, although she is bored by theory, is much more of a revolutionary than Winston. The Party's paranoid idealism and fascist cult of purity are threatened by the rival claims of the life of the body, and an easiness in – rather than a bullying of – the natural world. Orwell's characters do not enjoy themselves much or for very long, but it is almost always women who create what enjoyment there is in his stories, and each small moment of fun – 'Every joke is a tiny revolution' (*CW* xvi. 483) – is a victory won against denying authority. Julia's own private Bakhtinian carnival of promiscuity and gratified desire and coarse language makes a travesty of the scarlet sash of the Junior Anti-Sex League that she wears. She is also successful, and subversive, in breaking through the solitude created by the extreme alienation of life under Party rule. Trust, let alone intimacy, is inadvisable in Oceania, where there is no room for loyalty to anyone but Big Brother, and children are rewarded for spying on their parents and neighbours. It is to Winston's credit, and Julia's, that he does not betray Julia until the end of his torture, in Room 101. Once that last stubborn attachment is uprooted, he is released, returned to the harmless state of isolation and lovelessness where he began.

The Party is also dedicated to the destruction of individual memory, and therefore of individual identity (no identity without memory), as well as to the abolition, or rather rewriting, of history. Winston makes various attempts to retrieve his memories and connect his experience to the order of the past, though ironically enough he is not even sure whether the current year really is 1984. He recognizes, especially when he stumbles on concrete evidence that the 'confessions' of three notorious dissidents must be false, that a historical sense is an empowerment, which the rulers of Oceania have no intention of allowing to their citizens, preferring to keep them in a kind of historical suspension with no sense of an available past or future in whose name the present might be interpreted or even changed. A people denied history are also without agency. Like the subject peoples in Orwell's oriental writings, they are reduced to passivity as other people make their history for them (literally so, in the case of the Ministry of Truth).

This catalogue of what might be called the ideological opposition to totalitarianism comprises, without exception, the vital constituents of literary humanism, the writing in which Eric Blair located himself as George Orwell, and in particular of the discursive practice of the novel. In the novel is inscribed the history of private life – domestic, emotional, intellectual, bodily – in the context of an empirically known material world and a recognizable social environment. The novel is a unique act of individual language, produced and consumed in private and yet also the grounds for intersubjectivity, among its characters and between the novel and its readers, and perhaps a communication across years or centuries with the past. Experiments in life, as George Eliot called them, novels can be a testimony to individual and historical change, and to the discovery, formulation, and critique of values. Tyranny – left, right, or centre – cannot countenance any of these things, and is therefore incompatible with humanist literature. 'To be free', in the words of a contemporary novelist, 'you must first assume your right to freedom.'[6] Novels make that assumption, even or especially when they are about tyranny.

If totalitarianism were to become worldwide and permanent, Orwell wrote in 1941 at a time when it seemed possible that it might, 'what we have known as literature must come to an end' (*CW* xii. 503) – as indeed has happened in Oceania, where fiction has been reduced to a mechanical industrial process. Totalitarianism aspires to monologue, the reduction of all subjects to one voice and all minds to a single permissible point of view. But the novel is at best the opposite of this, a democratic form that revels in polyphony and insists on a hearing for different points of view. Orwell said he thought a novel should show credible individual characters acting on everyday motives and not merely undergoing strings of improbable adventures, and should have more than one character 'described from the inside and on the same level of probability' (*CW* xix. 350). Of course this is not actually a description of *Nineteen Eighty-Four*, and indeed Orwell himself never got round to writing a novel by this definition. However, as he says in 'Why I Write', circumstances dictate that an author does not always have the good fortune to be able to write what he would like. Yet it is certainly the novelistic elements of *Nineteen Eighty-Four* that stand in defiance of the inhumanity of the Party, and deny its triumph. While the Party is bent on remaking the world in its own grotesque and insane image, the novel itself is the humane discourse of opposition to the inhuman regime it imagines and contains. Although it tells a story that imagines the defeat of individual freedom, community, history, and conscience, it does so in a form of writing that continues to enact these very things every time it is read.

Notes

CHAPTER 3. ENGLAND

1. Raymond Williams, *Orwell*, Fontana Modern Masters, 3rd edn. (London: Fontana, 1991), 8.
2. He used the phrase twice, in 'Shooting an Elephant' (*CW* x. 501) and *The Road to Wigan Pier* (*RWP* 136).
3. In fact the fictional poem Gordon composes in the opening chapters of the novel appeared, disconcertingly, in the *Adelphi* in November 1935 (*CW* x. 402–3), over Blair's name, several months before the novel. It has acquired a title, 'St Andrew's Day, 1935', which is the day its fictional author started to compose it (*KAF* 3), though Comstock himself appears to have left it untitled.
4. See the 1946 essay 'Decline of the English Murder' (*CW* xviii. 108–10), with its argument that at least murders in a stable society mean something because they have 'strong emotions behind them'.
5. Gollancz's Preface is reproduced as an Appendix to the *Collected Works* version of *The Road to Wigan Pier* (*CW* v. 216–25) but is not in the Penguin edition. Gollancz has been much pilloried for publishing this preface, which in fact makes a number of good points, although in a context that makes them ethically dubious. Gollancz went on to reject *Homage to Catalonia*, publish *Coming Up for Air*, and reject *Animal Farm*.
6. *The English People* was part of a series called *Britain in Pictures* proposed by the Ministry of Information and, Orwell said, 'designed to "sell" Britain in the USA' (*CW* xix. 172).

CHAPTER 4. EUROPE

1. Peter Davison, *George Orwell: A Literary Life* (Basingstoke: Macmillan, 1996), 26.

2. 'The POUM . . . was one of those dissident Communist parties which have appeared in many countries in the last few years as a result of the opposition to Stalinism. . . . Numerically it was a small party, with not much influence outside Catalonia, and chiefly important because it contained an unusually high proportion of politically conscious members' (*HC* 202).
3. Orwell's essay 'Looking Back on the Spanish War' (*CW* xiii. 497–511), probably written in 1942, ends with his poem about the militiaman, 'The Italian soldier shook my hand'.
4. Christopher Hitchens, 'George Orwell and Raymond Williams', *Unacknowledged Legislation: Writers in the Public Sphere* (London: Verso, 2000), 32.
5. See *CW* xviii. 235–8, xix. 85–9, and Davison, *George Orwell*, 124–5.
6. Boxer's alphabetical agonies recall those of Joe Gargery in Dickens's *Great Expectations* and, in a different way, of Mr Ramsay in Virginia Woolf's *To the Lighthouse*.

CHAPTER 5. OCEANIA

1. John Newsinger, *Orwell's Politics* (London: Macmillan, 1999), 137.
2. See ibid. 54. Orwell was unaware that a security police report to the Tribunal for Espionage and High Treason, which has since come to light, described him and Eileen as 'rabid Trotskyists' (*CW* xi. 30–7). The report, written in Spanish, contains basic errors that would not be made by a Spaniard or a Catalan.
3. James Burnham, *The Struggle for the World* (London: Jonathan Cape, 1947), 147. Burnham's *The Managerial Revolution* (Harmondsworth: Penguin, 1945) had been published in the USA in 1941. It was reviewed in *Horizon* in 1942. Orwell first mentions it in January 1944 (*CW* xvi. 61).
4. See Roy Harris, 'The Misunderstanding of Newspeak', *TLS*, 6 Jan. 1984, 17.
5. Doublethink is itself particularly a hyperbolic transformation of the Communist and fellow-travelling party line in the Stalinist era (see e.g. *CW* xiii. 355–6), but more generally of 'a habit of mind which is extremely widespread, and perhaps always has been', which Orwell examined in 'In Front of Your Nose' in 1946 (*CW* xviii. 161–4).
6. Salman Rushdie, *In Good Faith* (London: Granta, 1990), 6.

Select Bibliography

WORKS BY GEORGE ORWELL

Collected Editions

The Collected Essays, Journalism and Letters, ed. Sonia Orwell and Ian Angus, 4 vols. (London: Secker & Warburg, 1968; Harmondsworth: Penguin, 1970).

The Complete Works of George Orwell, ed. Peter Davison, 20 vols. (London: Secker & Warburg, 1998).

Separate Editions

Down and Out in Paris and London (London: Gollancz, 1933; Harmondsworth: Penguin, 2001).

Burmese Days (New York: Harper & Brothers, 1934; London, Gollancz, 1935; Harmondsworth: Penguin, 1989).

A Clergyman's Daughter (London: Gollancz, 1935; Harmondsworth: Penguin, 1990).

Keep the Aspidistra Flying (London: Gollancz, 1936; Harmondsworth: Penguin, 1989).

The Road to Wigan Pier (London: Gollancz, 1937; London: Left Book Club, 1937; Harmondsworth: Penguin, 1989).

Homage to Catalonia (London: Secker & Warburg, 1938; Harmondsworth: Penguin, 1989).

Coming Up for Air (London: Gollancz, 1939; Harmondsworth: Penguin, 2001).

Inside the Whale and Other Essays (London: Gollancz, 1940).

The Lion and the Unicorn (London: Secker & Warburg, 1941).

Talking to India, ed. and introduced by Orwell (London: Allen and Unwin, 1943).

Animal Farm (London: Secker & Warburg, 1945; Harmondsworth: Penguin, 1989).

Critical Essays (London: Secker & Warburg, 1946).

The English People (London: Collins, 1947).

Nineteen Eighty-Four (London: Secker & Warburg, 1949; Harmondsworth: Penguin, 1989).

The War Broadcasts, ed. W. J. West (Harmondsworth: Penguin, 1987).

The War Commentaries, ed. W. J. West (Harmondsworth: Penguin, 1987).

BIOGRAPHY

Crick, Bernard, *George Orwell: A Life*, 3rd edn. (Harmondsworth: Penguin, 1981).

Meyers, Jeffrey, *Orwell: Wintry Conscience of a Generation* (New York: Norton, 2000).

Shelden, Michael, *Orwell: The Authorized Biography* (London: Heinemann, 1991).

Stansky, Peter, and Abrahams, William, *The Unknown Orwell and Orwell: The Transformation*, combined edn. (Stanford, Calif.: Stanford University Press, 1994).

Wadhams, Stephen, *Remembering Orwell* (Harmondsworth: Penguin, 1984).

CRITICISM

Baneth-Nouailhetas, Emilienne, 'George Orwell and the "White Man's Burden" ', *Commonwealth: Essays and Studies*, 17/1 (1991), 32–9. A brief study of Orwell and empire.

Beddoe, Dierdre, 'Hindrances and Help-Meets: Women in the Writings of George Orwell', in Christopher Norris (ed.), *Inside the Myth: Orwell, Views from the Left* (London: Lawrence & Wishart, 1984), 139–54. A useful critical review of the representation of women in Orwell's fiction and journalism.

Brent, Harry, ' "Bullets Hurt, Corpses Stink": George Orwell and the Language of Warfare', in William Lutz (ed.), *Beyond Nineteen Eighty-Four: Doublespeak in a Post-Orwellian Age* (Urbana, Ill.: National Council of Teachers of English, 1989), 99–110. Lively account of Orwell as a war writer.

Briggs, Asa, *The History of Broadcasting in the United Kingdom*, iii. *The War of Words* (London: Oxford University Press, 1970). The institutional history, in which Orwell plays a small part.

Buddicom, Jacinta, 'The Young Eric', in Miriam Gross (ed.), *The World of George Orwell* (London: Weidenfeld & Nicolson, 1971), 1–8. Reminiscences of Eric Blair's childhood friend.

Calder, Jenni, *Animal Farm & Nineteen Eighty-Four* (Milton Keynes: Open University Press, 1987). A guide to the two novels with a useful self-study discussion format.

Campbell, Beatrix, 'Orwell – Paterfamilias or Big Brother?', in Graham Holderness, Bryan Loughrey, and Nahem Vousaf (eds.), *George Orwell*, New Casebooks (New York: St Martins Press, 1998), 64–75. Offers a provocative critique of Orwell's 'big-brotherly' representation of the working class as both masculine and mindless.

Connelly, Mark, *Orwell and Gissing* (New York: Peter Lang, 1997). An examination of one of Orwell's strongest literary relationships.

Coombes, John, 'A New Dissection of Orwell's Elephant', in Francis Barker *et al.* (eds.), *Practices in Literature and Politics* (Colchester: University of Essex, 1979), 245–57. Compelling exposition of 'Shooting an Elephant' as a radically dialogic text.

Crick, Bernard, 'Orwell and the Business of Biography', in William Roger Louis (ed.), *More Adventures with Britannia: Personalities, Politics and Culture in Britain* (Austin, Tex.: University of Texas Press, 1998), 151–68. Shrewd and amusing account of the tribulations of Orwell's first biographer.

Cunningham, Valentine, *British Writers of the Thirties* (Oxford: Oxford University Press, 1988). An excellent, absorbing and comprehensive cultural history, which provides a professional and political context for Orwell's work.

Davison, Peter, *George Orwell: A Literary Life* (Basingstoke: Macmillan, 1996). Tells the story of Orwell's professional life, including his relations with employers, editors, publishers, censors, correspondents, readers and other writers. Written by the editor of *The Complete Works of George Orwell.*

Dentith, Simon, ' "The Journalists do the Shouting": Orwell and Propaganda', in Graham Holderness, Bryan Loughrey, and Nahem Vousaf (eds.), *George Orwell*, New Casebooks (New York: St Martins Press, 1998), 203–27. Goes beyond Orwell's reputation for honesty to examine his alertness to the rhetorical and pragmatic interests of writing.

Eagleton, Terry, *Exiles and Emigrés: Studies in Modern Literature* (London: Chatto & Windus, 1970). The chapter on Orwell argues that his characters can neither accept nor disengage from a hated social system. Like most Marxist criticism, sees Orwell's political critique as seriously compromised.

Ehrenfeld, David, 'The Roots of Prophecy: Orwell and Nature', *Beginning Again: People and Nature in the New Millennium* (New York: Oxford University Press, 1993), 8–28. An appreciation by a biologist of Orwell's admiration of environments where people and nature interact in a positive way.

Elson, Brigid, 'Crucial Devices: The Role of the Media in Orwell, Waugh, Hitchcock and Antonioni', *Antigonish Review* (Summer–Autumn 1995), 133–41. Useful consideration is given to Orwell's representations of journalists and journalism.

Fleay, C., and Sanders, M. L., 'Looking into the Abyss: George Orwell at the BBC', *Journal of Contemporary History*, 24/3 (July 1989), 503–18. An attempt at a historical assessment of Orwell's involvement in broadcasting.

Fowler, Roger, *The Language of George Orwell* (Basingstoke: Macmillan, 1995). A critical-linguistic study with a Bakhtinian focus, full of insights but ultimately a little disappointing.

Gervais, David, *Literary Englands: Versions of 'Englishness' in Modern Writing* (Cambridge: Cambridge University Press, 1993). Orwell is one of the subjects in this examination of a topic of growing contemporary interest.

Goodall, Peter, 'The Politics of Nature: Pastoral Scenes in George Orwell's Novels', *AUMLA (Journal of the Australian Universities Language and Literature Association)*, 68 (1987), 188–206. Examines the political dimension of Orwell's uses of pastoral.

—— '"Was the So-called Melon Actually a Pumpkin?": Orwell and the Problem of Realism', *AUMLA (Journal of the Australian Universities Language and Literature Association)*, 75 (1991), 3–20. A thoughtful contribution to the debate about realism, representation and truth in Orwell's work.

Greenblatt, Stephen, *Three Modern Satirists: Waugh, Orwell and Huxley* (New Haven: Yale University Press, 1965). Greenblatt's first book contains a stylish account of Orwell's satire.

Gross, John, 'Imperial Attitudes', in Miriam Gross (ed.), *The World of George Orwell* (London: Weidenfeld & Nicolson, 1971), 31–8. Gives a broadly sympathetic account of Orwell's developing views of the empire.

Gross, Miriam (ed.), *The World of George Orwell* (London: Weidenfeld & Nicolson, 1971). The popular format of this book contains some indispensable reminiscences of Orwell.

Guha, Ranajit, 'Not at Home in Empire', *Critical Inquiry*, 23/3 (1997), 482–93. An examination of location and alienation in empire from the foremost practitioner of subaltern studies historiography.

Gupta, Partha Sarathi, *Radio and the Raj 1921–47* (Calcutta: K. P. Bagchi for the Centre for Studies in Social Sciences, 1995). Contains some useful documentary details about the BBC and All-India Radio, censorship, and wartime propaganda.

Harris, Roy, 'The Misunderstanding of Newspeak', *TLS*, 6 Jan. 1984, 17. A classic and timely statement on the linguistic myth of Newspeak.

Hitchens, Christopher, 'George Orwell and Raymond Williams', *Unacknowledged Legislation: Writers in the Public Sphere* (London: Verso, 2000), 26–43. Hitchens mounts a spirited defence of Orwell's life and writing from doctrinaire attacks by Williams and others.

—— *Orwell's Victory* (London: Allen Lane, The Penguin Press, 2002). A lively vindication of Orwell by a contemporary contrarian.

Holderness, Graham, Loughrey, Bryan, and Vousaf, Nahem (eds.), *George Orwell*, New Casebooks (New York: St Martins Press, 1998). An indispensable collection of a dozen important recent essays, with an excellent introduction.

Hollis, Christopher, *A Study of George Orwell: The Man and his Works* (London: Hollis & Carter, 1956). A friendly early assessment of the career and writing.

Hunter, Lynette, *George Orwell: The Search for a Voice* (Milton Keynes: Open University Press, 1984). This dense and complex book is one of the most subtle and penetrating critical engagements with Orwell's language. It reflects on questions of modality, authority, pragmatics, representation and writing, as these recur throughout Orwell's career.

—— 'Blood and Marmalade: Negotiations between the State and the Domestic in George Orwell's Early Novels', in Keith Williams and Steven Matthews (eds.), *Rewriting the Thirties: Modernism and After* (London: Longman, 1997), 202–16. A difficult but rewarding essay on ideology and naturalization in Orwell's fiction.

Ingle, Stephen, *George Orwell: A Political Life* (Manchester: Manchester University Press, 1993). An accessible, brisk and sympathetic study of Orwell as a political figure.

—— 'The Anti-Imperialism of George Orwell', in Graham Holderness, Bryan Loughrey, and Nahem Vousaf (eds.), *George Orwell*, New Casebooks (New York: St Martins Press, 1998), 228–48. Examines Orwell's attempt to define the proper relationship between the rulers and the ruled through his fiction.

Islam, Shamsul, 'George Orwell and the Raj', *World Literature Written in English* 21:2 (1982), 341–7. An early attempt to deal with Orwell's ambivalence about empire.

Joseph, John E., 'Orwell on Language and Politics', in John E. Joseph, Nigel Love, and Talbot J. Taylor, *Landmarks in Linguistic Thought II: The Western Tradition in the Twentieth Century* (London: Routledge, 2001), 29–42. Definitive essay on Orwell as a thinker about language, in his political and literary essays and in *Nineteen Eighty-Four*.

Kerr, Douglas, 'Orwell, Animals and the East', *Essays in Criticism*, 49/3 (1999), 234–55. Argues that Orwell's narratives work out their complex attitudes to the Orient through the depiction of animals and the natural world.

Lea, Daniel, *George Orwell, Animal Farm, Nineteen Eighty-Four* (London: Icon Books, 2001). A good introduction to Orwell's two most popular books, their reception and interpretation.

Lee, Robert A., *Orwell's Fiction* (Notre Dame, Ind.: University of Notre Dame Press, 1969). A useful early but not always accurate study of Orwell's fiction as a whole.

Lukacs, John, Said, Edward, and Graff, Gerald, 'The Legacy of Orwell: A Discussion', *Salmagundi*, 70/1 (1986), 121–8. A debate among three eminent critics about Orwell's political and literary importance.

Marks, Peter, 'The Ideological Eye-Witness: An Examination of the Eye-Witness in Two Works by George Orwell', in Philip Shaw and Peter Stockwell (eds.), *Subjectivity and Literature from the Romantics to the Present Day* (London: Pinter, 1991), 85–92. Another textual study of the tricky question of modality, authenticity and truth-telling in Orwell's writing.

—— 'Where He Wrote: Periodicals and the Essays of George Orwell', *Twentieth Century Literature*, 41/4 (1995), 266–83. This absorbing essay shows how Orwell adjusted his discourse to different publication outlets and different readerships.

Matthews, Brian, 'Understanding George Orwell: The War Broadcasts and War Commentaries', *Quadrant*, 30/10 (1986), 35–9. An early account of Orwell as broadcaster, still of interest although overtaken by more recent scholarship.

Maung Htin Aung, 'George Orwell and Burma', in Miriam Gross (ed.), *The World of George Orwell* (London: Weidenfeld & Nicolson, 1971), 19–30. The distinguished Burmese scholar's account of Orwell's career in and writing about colonial Burma.

Meyers, Jeffrey, *A Reader's Guide to George Orwell* (London: Thames & Hudson, 1975). A serviceable reference guide, still of some interest.

—— (ed.), *George Orwell: The Critical Heritage* (London: Routledge & Kegan Paul, 1975). An invaluable history of how Orwell was seen by his contemporaries.

Meyers, Valerie, *George Orwell*, Macmillan Modern Novelists (Basingstoke: Macmillan, 1991). An introductory study of the fiction.

Newsinger, John, *Orwell's Politics* (London: Macmillan, 1999). A very useful study of the development of Orwell's political ideas and beliefs, from his early dissatisfaction with empire to his anti-Stalinist socialism.

Norris, Christopher (ed.), *Inside the Myth: Orwell, Views from the Left* (London: Lawrence & Wishart, 1984). A collection of mostly hostile criticism made in 1984. There was a flood of Orwell criticism in this year.

Patai, Daphne, *The Orwell Mystique: A Study in Male Ideology* (Amherst, Mass.: University of Massachusetts Press, 1984). Orwell is seen in this book as representing and perpetuating a world governed by masculine values and interests.

Rodden, John, *The Politics of Literary Reputation: The Making and Claiming of 'St George' Orwell* (Oxford: Oxford University Press, 1989). Rodden examines Orwell as a cultural sign with changing meanings, in this detailed and fascinating account of the ideological battleground of Orwell's reputation.

—— '"A Sexist After All"?: The Feminists' Orwell', *New Orleans Review*, 17/1 (1990), 33–46. An attempt is made to adjudicate the feminist quarrel with Orwell.

Rorty, Richard, 'The Last Intellectual in Europe', in Graham Holderness, Bryan Loughrey, and Nahem Vousaf (eds.), *George Orwell*, New Casebooks (New York: St Martins Press, 1998), 139–60. An assessment of the importance of the last two novels in creating our understanding of the world we inhabit. Rorty concludes that Orwell's description of the political situation of the twentieth century is 'as useful as any we possess'.

Rose, Jonathan (ed.), *The Revised Orwell* (East Lansing, Mich.: Michigan State University Press, 1992). Bibliographical studies.

—— 'The Invisible Sources of *Nineteen Eighty-Four*', *Journal of Popular Culture*, 26/1 (1992), 93–107. Part of a substantial literature on the origins of Orwell's last novel.

Ross, William T., 'Pacifism vs. Patriotism: The Case of George Orwell', *Weber Studies*, 12/2 (1995), 54–66. Stages a debate between ideas in which Orwell embraced the less intellectually fashionable option.

Rossi, John, 'Orwell and Patriotism', *Contemporary Review*, 261/1519 (1992), 95–8. A lucid exploration of this complex subject in its political context.

Sandison, Alan, *George Orwell: After 1984* (Basingstoke: Macmillan, 1986). A re-issue of the fine critical study first published in 1974 as *The Last Man in Europe*.

Seed, David, 'Disorientation and Commitment in the Fiction of Empire: Kipling and Orwell', *Dutch Quarterly Review of Anglo-American Letters*, 14/4 (1984), 269–80. Discusses Orwell's struggles to dramatize adequately his hostility to empire.

Stewart, D. H., 'Shooting Elephants Right', *Southern Review*, 22/1 (1986), 86–92. Compares Orwell to Kipling, to Orwell's disadvantage.

Walzer, Michael, 'George Orwell's England', in Graham Holderness, Bryan Loughrey, and Nahem Vousaf (eds.), *George Orwell*, New Casebooks (New York: St Martins Press, 1998), 182–202. This essay makes a powerful argument for Orwell as democrat, committed to the transfer of power in England to ordinary men and women and to the creation of an open, plain-spoken politics.

West, W. J., *The Larger Evils: Nineteen Eighty-Four: The Truth behind the Satire* (Edinburgh: Canongate Press, 1992). Orwell's experience with censorship, and the warnings of *Nineteen Eighty-Four*, are part of this book's passionate argument about surveillance and state control.

Williams, Keith, 'Post/Modern Documentary: Orwell, Agee and the New Reportage', in Keith Williams and Steven Matthews, *Rewriting the Thirties: Modernism and After* (London: Longman, 1997), 163–81. Orwell's work, especially *The Road to Wigan Pier* and *Homage to Catalonia*, examined as part of the 'documentary' project of the thirties.

—— and Matthews, Steven, *Rewriting the Thirties: Modernism and After* (London: Longman, 1997). Plenty of useful context for the 'low, dishonest decade'.

Raymond Williams, *Orwell*, Fontana Modern Masters, 3rd edn. (London: Fontana, 1991), 8. An important episode in the great socialist critic's long quarrel with Orwell, in which Orwell's championing of justice and equality is ultimately felt to be undermined by his rootlessess and pessimism.

Young, John Wesley, *Totalitarian Language: Orwell's Newspeak and its Nazi and Communist Antecedents* (Charlottesville, Va.: University Press of Virginia, 1991). Argues for *Nineteen Eighty-Four*'s account of the corruption of language as an important contribution to political theory.

Index